A Guide to Your Examination of
Teaching the Integrated Language Arts

by Shane Templeton

The good teachers I had were interested in *me*, a perennially over-active student from kindergarten through high school who floundered in math from fractions to functions. Whenever stationary, however, I was reading, writing—and, of course, talking! Some of my teachers, and they were very special ones indeed, let me teach *them*.

I believe these are monumentally exciting times for language arts education. If we do it right, we can help our children come to understand themselves in deeply consequential ways. Through reading, writing, discussion, and critical reflection, they can come to make better sense of sharing those constants and those strategies about teaching the language arts that, over the last two decades, I have been so fortunate and honored to explore with many wonderful present and future teachers.

Audience and Purpose

Teaching the Integrated Language Arts has been written for preservice elementary school teachers. It is intended for a first course in language arts as well as for courses in which reading and language arts theory and methods are combined. The book can also serve as a foundations text for inservice teachers returning to pursue further graduate work; in this capacity it can familiarize teachers with the new thinking and developments in writing, reading, and language. For both of these groups of students, the book is intended to serve as a practical classroom resource. The text can also provide a solid grounding in the language arts—the core of the elementary curriculum—for students in educational leadership and administration who are doing coursework in curriculum and instruction.

The book's fundamental premise is that elementary students must be engaged in frequent reading, writing, and speaking throughout all areas of an integrated curriculum. Furthermore, this integrated curriculum should be based upon and occur within a real-world context that involves significant exposure to literature.

Knowledgeable teachers play a seminal role in orchestrating this involvement and in helping students to think critically. Running throughout this book is the firm belief that all teachers *can* and *must* become knowledgeable about the dynamic enterprise of teaching. Always considering the needs of the developing teacher, this text establishes an empathetic tone, anticipating and addressing directly the concerns of a novice and providing considerable practical information about the what, when, and how of teaching the integrated language arts.

Coverage

Teaching the Integrated Language Arts presents applied instructional strategies and activities and the theory behind those applications in thirteen chapters. Each of the language arts is presented and discussed with the other language arts in mind so that integration is shown in operation within every chapter.

Because teachers' instructional decisions can be informed by their knowledge of both children's language and cognitive development and of the process behind each of the language arts, background discussions and illustrations of both development and process are woven throughout the book. Equally important in the modern world is a teacher's understanding of different cultures and the special needs of diverse student populations. Thus, diversity is a theme that underlies instructional presentation in all chapters.

The first three chapters lay much of the theoretical groundwork. **Chapter 1** defines the important terms, sets up the framework of an integrated language arts curriculum, and describes the contexts in and out of school that affect children's development. **Chapter 2** presents an overview of the important concepts in the development and functioning of language and cognition, primarily during the important preschool years. The chapter emphasizes the role of social interaction in helping children *construct* their understandings. **Chapter 3** briefly presents a historical overview of spoken and written language and then concentrates on the development of the English language. The chapter suggests that even a casual familiarity with this historical picture should be of benefit to the classroom teacher, but more important, this type of understanding should help the teacher explore the history of language and its relevance to vocabulary, usage, and spelling with the elementary school student.

Chapter 4 covers organization and management within the classroom and describes the context in which integrated language arts instruction occurs effectively. This information is presented early in the text in order to give students a realistic framework within which to fit subsequent instructional information; the chapter could also be valuable used later in the course. The chapter provides in-depth discussions and an extended illustrative example of the kind of elementary classroom that provides a predictable instructional environment fostering student independence and critical thinking.

Chapter 5 addresses the oral language foundations of the language arts. The chapter demonstrates how to facilitate students' development in these areas and explains how listening, speaking, and creative dramatics establish a natural foundation for instruction and development in writing and reading.

Chapters 6, 7, and 8 work together to explore in considerable depth the topics of writing and reading. First, **Chapter 6** offers a developmental perspective on each of writing and reading and on the interaction of these two processes. Then, **Chapter 7** treats the writing process in detail. All stages—prewriting through sharing and publishing—are discussed, and specific guidelines for conferencing, questioning, and facilitating different types of writing are presented. Next, **Chapter 8** examines the nature of reading comprehension and word knowledge, from an interactive viewpoint. Guidelines for teaching strategic reading of narrative and expository texts are offered. This chapter can serve as either a comprehensive introduction to reading for the neophyte or as an excellent review for students who have already taken a course in the teaching of reading.

Chapter 9 weaves together all the instructional pieces presented thus far and demonstrates how reading, writing, and oral language can be integrated within a literature-based language arts curriculum. After providing brief overviews of the different categories of children's literature, the chapter walks students through the transition from a more traditional type of language arts classroom to a predominantly literature-based classroom. Literature response activities are offered, culminating with the presentation of two representative thematic or literature-based units.

The premise behind **Chapter 10,** which treats both vocabulary and spelling instruction, is that the topics of vocabulary and spelling are linked by a spelling-meaning connection. Within the context of the other language arts, strategies for the productive exploration of words are presented. **Chapter 11** discusses instruction of grammar, mechanics, usage, and handwriting. These traditional aspects of the language arts are presented in a functional context so that they make sense to students and have a purpose.

Chapter 12 offers a general overview of assessment and evaluation. Portfolio assessment, informal observation, other types of informal assessment, and the changing nature of formal tests are all explored. **Chapter 13** concludes the text by addressing the theme of student diversity within the elementary school classroom. The chapter is aimed at helping teachers develop awareness of the needs of multicultural and special education learners. The chapter's underlying premise is that effective teaching of special needs students is based on appropriate application of excellent regular education strategies and activities.

Features

The text includes a number of special features to help students construct their understandings of the content and apply these understandings.

■ *Focusing Questions* at the beginning of each chapter address major concepts that students should acquire as they read the chapter.

■ *Chapter Opening Quotations and Introductions* open each chapter and help orient students to the content while providing a realistic perspective of the importance of the topics.

■ *Classroom Examples* are set off throughout the book to illustrate teaching in action. They are an integral part of the chapter and provide real modeling of effective teaching strategies for the reader.

■ *Build Your Teaching Resources* are annotated bibliographies that appear directly within the chapters and that list both children's literature and professional resources.

■ *Expand Your Teaching Repertoire* lists provide in-depth walk-throughs of instructional strategies and activities intended for use in the elementary classroom.

■ *At the Teacher's Desk*, set-off "advice boxes" that run throughout the chapters, offer observations about a wide range of teaching and learning issues, and provide a forum for the author to share personal perspectives and insights about the topics at hand.

■ A *Concluding Perspective*, summaries at the ends of the chapters, not only summarize the contents of the chapter but also act to coalesce the material and to present it as a springboard for ensuing topics.

■ *Appendices* A through E conclude the book. Appendix A is a resource for Chapter 10 and should be referred to during the reading of that chapter; it lists important structural elements (prefixes, suffixes, stems) in words. Appendices B, C, and D present scope and sequence charts for the teaching of grammar, mechanics, and usage. Appendix E offers a selection of recommended computer software that effectively complements language arts instruction.

Instructor's Resource Manual with Test Items

This manual is divided into two parts. The first part includes for each chapter a lecture discussion outline; a prose summary of the chapter's contents; a list of supplementary discussion topics; and a compilation of relevant student activities. In addition, two sets of multiple-choice test questions, with separate answer sheets, are provided for each chapter. Part Two consists of fourteen masters that can be converted into transparencies and projected and/or can be reproduced and distributed to students.

Instructor's Resource Manual
with Test Items

TEACHING THE INTEGRATED LANGUAGE ARTS

TEACHING THE INTEGRATED LANGUAGE ARTS

Shane Templeton

INSTRUCTOR'S RESOURCE MANUAL
WITH TEST ITEMS

Jerry Converse
California State University, Chico

HOUGHTON MIFFLIN COMPANY   BOSTON

Dallas • Geneva, Illinois • Palo Alto • Princeton, New Jersey

CONTENTS

PREFACE

This Instructor's Resource Manual has been designed to assist instructors who are using *Teaching the Integrated Language Arts*.

The manual is divided into two parts. Part One, "Instructional Guide and Test Items," offers teaching suggestions and test items for each chapter. Part Two, "Instructional Masters," offers a set of fourteen masters that can be converted into transparencies and projected and/or can be reproduced and distributed to students.

Chapters in Part One correspond to the text. For each chapter several teaching aids are provided. First, there is a Lecture Discussion Outline, which lists in outline format all the chapter headings. Next a prose Summary synthesizes the major concepts and issues of the chapter. The instructor may use each of these sections to quickly review the contents of the chapter.

Third, a Supplementary Discussion Topics section presents a list of additional topic ideas related to those treated in the chapter itself. These ideas can act as a springboard for class discussions. The fourth section, Student Activities, offers a list of activities that students may pursue in or out of class to extend their learning and understanding of the chapter material.

Finally, for each chapter, A and B versions of a fifteen-item multiple-choice test are provided. An Answer Key for each test appears at the end of Part One.

Part Two includes fourteen masters, each of which is based on charts, diagrams, or content coverage in the text. A set of guidelines precedes the individual masters and offers suggestions for ways in which the masters can augment presentation of the textbook material.

Instructor's Resource Manual
with Test Items

TEACHING THE INTEGRATED LANGUAGE ARTS

PART ONE

INSTRUCTIONAL GUIDE
AND TEST ITEMS

The Language Arts: Content and Context

LECTURE DISCUSSION OUTLINE

CONTENT: WHAT ARE THE LANGUAGE ARTS?

Thought and Language: The Bases of the Language Arts

> Thought
> Language

CONTEXT: THE MODERN WORLD

Our Multicultural Society

Our Information Society

CONTENT AND CONTEXT: INTERACTIONS WITH INFORMATION

Print

Electronic Media and Film

> Television
> Film
> Radio
> Computers

Social Relationships

IMPLICATIONS FOR THE DYNAMIC TEACHING OF THE LANGUAGE ARTS

SUMMARY

The language arts are the tools humans use to communicate and to understand themselves and the world in which they live. Language arts teachers should help students learn how to use these tools effectively, so they become competent in applying reading, writing, speaking, and listening to their own learning, creativity, and social development. In order to do this, teachers need to understand how thought and language are the bases of the language arts. They must also be aware of the various contexts in which language arts are applied.

Humans are meaning seekers. After organizing and categorizing experiences, we interpret the information and make judgements. From this process we learn. Topical knowledge is a collection of facts and/or information. Procedural knowledge is how we go about learning or studying. Self-knowledge is our awareness of our learning processes and our ability to monitor them (metacognition). Teachers want to distinguish among the three types in order to develop students who use all three kinds of knowledge. Only when the learner transforms all three kinds of knowledge, does s/he think critically. If we carry this kind of thinking to teaching language, it has certain implications. We must teach children how to apply their knowledge of language—to read and write as well as communicate effectively and consequentially in written and spoken language.

The context in which students and teachers function influences how they will teach the language arts. Context includes not only the school and classroom, but also the cultural heritage of the students. Teachers must be sensitive to the cultural diversity among their students. Cultural background shapes the knowledge and language a student brings to the classroom and influences how the student learns and functions in the classroom. Student knowledge and language are also shaped by social interaction with peers and adults, electronic media, and print.

Teachers need to create a learning environment where meaningful speaking, listening, reading, and writing are first and foremost. Freedom to communicate and to take risks should be developed and encouraged. With guidance and proper instruction, students will develop the communication skills which allow them to become independent learners and thinkers.

SUPPLEMENTARY DISCUSSION TOPICS

1. Do a semantic map with "language content." Moving from specifics to categories should lead to some interesting comments or discussions. You might start with the four branches of the language arts as your categories.

2. Share and discuss some of the ideas from the cinquain poems that were written outside of class. (See student activity 1.)

3. Design one or several short lessons for the class that demonstrate one of the three kinds of knowledge. Following the lesson, discuss what made it what it was—topical, procedural, or self-knowledge.

4. Have students share a classroom experience, where children used meaningful communicative language. Discuss what made it "meaningful" communication, rather than "contrived" language. An example would be children writing to the Canadian government for information for a report versus copying something from an encyclopedia.

5. Take a quick cultural inventory of students in the class. Share the information and discuss how the variety of backgrounds influences how the learners will perceive the learning situation.

6. Structure a discussion by saying, "Remember when you first entered college. How did you feel? What did you expect?" Relate these experiences and feelings to how a child might feel coming to school from a home environment.

STUDENT ACTIVITIES

1. Have each student write a cinquain poem on the chapter and share some in class, as your entry to a discussion. Your cinquain could follow this pattern:

   Main idea of chapter (one word)
   Synthesis of the parts (two words)
   Affective reaction to the author's ideas (three words)
   How the student will use the idea in teaching (four words)
   Synonym (one word)

   An example:

   Tools
   Content/Context
   Enlightened about complexities
   Emphasize communication over knowledge
   Communication

2. Have the students interview a teacher about the variety of cultural backgrounds s/he has in the classroom. Write a one-page summary.

3. Assign a two-page summary or analysis of an article in a professional journal or from a chapter of a book, about cultural influences on learning.

4. Have the students construct a three-column chart labeled Topical Knowledge, Procedural Knowledge, and Self-Knowledge. Under each category describe at least three personal classroom experiences which demonstrate that type of knowledge.

5. Ask the students to talk with a bilingual teacher about the culture of her population for insights into gaining a better understanding of that culture. Have them submit a one-page summary of their "findings."

EXAM 1-A

1. To conclude an emergency vehicle is moving closer, on the basis of hearing a siren, demonstrates our ability to

   A. interpret.
   B. organize.
   C. judge.
   D. all of the above.

2. Critical thinking is the application of

   A. topical knowledge.
   B. procedural knowledge.
   C. self knowledge.
   D. all of the above.

3. The four language arts are listening, speaking, .

   A. judgment, and reading.
   B. spelling, and writing.
   C. reading, and writing.
   D. critical thinking, and reading.

4. Four major American subcultures include African, Hispanic, _____, and _____.

   A. Greek, Roman.
   B. Roman, Jewish.
   C. Asian, Native American.
   D. Hmong, Asian.

5. According to the text, which one of the following media is the most pervasive?

   A. Television
   B. Cinema
   C. Print
   D. Computers

6. A teacher can use television positively by

   A. bringing televisions into the classroom.
   B. limiting the time of viewing.
   C. limiting the kinds of programs.
   D. structuring the viewing and discussion.

7. A distinctive difference between reading and the other language arts is that when you read,

   A. you must analyze information more quickly.
   B. your images are controlled by the author.
   C. you control the rate and type of information processed.
   D. it is harder to reflect and analyze.

8. Teaching students the mechanics of stream erosion, then asking them to figure out ways to prevent or reduce erosion, represents

   A. transformation of topical knowledge.
   B. transformation of self-knowledge.
   C. transformation of procedural knowledge.
   D. transformation of spatial knowledge.

9. The acquisition of language skills is

   A. the product of our meaning-making nature.
   B. begun as early as first grade.
   C. a simple process.
   D. all of the above.

10. In a learning environment that encourages freedom to communicate,

    A. students have the right to talk at any time.
    B. organization and control are *not* needed.
    C. organization and control *are* needed.
    D. students are *not* willing to take risks.

11. Students need to be taught to be knowledgeable consumers of information in order to

    A. be more intelligent.
    B. obtain better grades.
    C. be in control of their decisions.
    D. be admitted into college.

12. Because there is so much more information available now than in previous years and because we have greater access to that information, we

    A. need more skill in the language arts than our predecessors did.
    B. need less skill in the language arts than our predecessors did.
    C. are smarter than our predecessors.
    D. are more informed than our predecessors.

13. Social contexts in the classroom

    A. should always be structured by the teacher.
    B. provide the situation in which learning occurs.
    C. are inappropriate, and should be discouraged by the teacher.
    D. are not influenced by other contexts.

14. The popularity of "blues" music is a form of

    A. a minority's ways being incorporated into the predominant culture.
    B. immigrant society losing identity with its roots.
    C. the influence of our melting pot on immigrant societies.
    D. assimilating the values of the predominant culture.

15. Sentence diagramming is justified by those who think language is taught as

    A. a tool.
    B. an art.
    C. reasoning.
    D. "busy work."

1. Reading one's science report to the class is an example of language as

   A. an art.
   B. "busy work."
   C. a tool.
   D. reasoning.

2. As categorizing beings, we

   A. interpret.
   B. organize.
   C. value.
   D. all of the above.

3. If you have students list character traits and give supporting information from the text, you are working on

   A. topical knowledge.
   B. self knowledge.
   C. transformed knowledge.
   D. procedural knowledge.

4. Celebrating St. Patrick's Day is an application of

   A. religious freedom.
   B. cultural literacy.
   C. Celtic prejudice.
   D. ethnic discrimination.

5. You will teach critical analysis of information, because you want your students to

   A. be better informed.
   B. be smarter.
   C. know more.
   D. have the potential to overwhelm.

6. The popularity of the Bible is an example of

   A. the persuasive power of print.
   B. the need for interpretation skills.
   C. the permanence of printed materials.
   D. an unexplained miracle.

7. According to the text, effective teachers

   A. facilitate meaningful interactions among students.
   B. help develop a commitment to self-learning.
   C. develop an understanding of how language and thinking affect learning.
   D. all of the above.

8. Having students read a book about George Washington Carver and then discuss his contributions to farming and the food industry demonstrates

   A. the application of language arts in content subjects.
   B. motivation for teaching language arts.
   C. evaluation of reading comprehension.
   D. lower-level thinking skills.

9. According to the text, microcomputers in the classroom are most functional for

   A. drill and practice.
   B. word processing.
   C. testing.
   D. data management.

10. The language and knowledge children bring with them to school are shaped by

    A. print.
    B. electronic media.
    C. social interaction with peers and adults.
    D. all of the above.

11. Participating in a debate is an example of using language as

    A. an art form.
    B. drill and practice.
    C. a tool.
    D. a content subject.

12. The cultural heritage of a student

    A. influences how the child will act in school.
    B. determines if the child will be a successful learner.
    C. determines if the child will have learning problems.
    D. none of the above.

13. If a student asks you a question you cannot an

    A. tell the student to use the encyclope   tion.
    B. direct the student to a person wh
    C. admit that you don't know and   ogether.
    D. have the student "teach" you ho   swer.

14. If teachers want to use children's televi   viewing in a positive way, they should

    A. show current episodes as rewards.
    B. relate instruction to television experiences of the children.
    C. make the children read *TV Guide*.
    D. show the World Series in October.

15. The four language arts are

    A. reading, spelling, listening, and writing.
    B. reading, writing, listening, and speaking.
    C. reading, writing, drama, and listening.
    D. reading, English, drama, and listening.

Thought and Language

LECTURE DISCUSSION OUTLINE

FOUNDATIONS OF THOUGHT AND LANGUAGE: THE COMMUNICATION POTENTIAL

Thought and Language: Some Common Principles

THOUGHT AND ITS DEVELOPMENT

Metacognition

LANGUAGE AND ITS DEVELOPMENT

What Is To Be Learned?

Semantics
Syntax
Phonology

The Preschool Years

Birth to Two Years
Two Years to Five Years
The Contexts of Early Language Learning
Written Language in Oral Language Development.
Metalinguistic Awareness

SUMMARY

If teachers are to develop fully the communicative potential of children, they need a basic understanding of how thought and language develop in the preschool child. The underlying processes used in their construction are essentially the same as those the child will continue to use throughout life. That initial understanding provides strong implications for how to set up the learning environment and what teachers can expect to accomplish. First and foremost, children are meaning makers. They construct their knowledge of the world through hypothesis testing. Concepts are set up, differentiated, integrated, and formed as schemas. Knowledge in young children, however, is based primarily on their physical actions upon their world, centering on one aspect at a time. As they interact with their environment, their schemas become more finely differentiated and hierarchically organized. By the time children enter school, they are able to cognitively decenter, although until age 11 or 12 their abstract thinking must be based on concrete experience. For most children, metacognition becomes important during the intermediate grades.

As with cognitive development, preschool children learn language by interacting with the people in their environment. They make adjustments in their language according to the social context in which it occurs. Children tacitly learn the rules of semantics, syntax, and phonology because they constantly strive for meaning in their communication. Beginning with attaching labels to important people and things, young children soon progress to expressing simple relationships. With more experience, telegraphic speech occurs followed by the inclusion of function words, inflectional endings, plurals, and interrogatives in their speech. By the time children are five, most of them have completed the greater part of basic language acquisition. They have the skills not only to act upon their world, but also to reflect upon those actions.

When children enter school, they have developed extensive language and cognitive skills. With an awareness and understanding of the foundation children bring to school, it is the teacher's role to help them expand and elaborate their thinking and language and realize their communicative potential.

SUPPLEMENTARY DISCUSSION TOPICS

1. Develop a semantic map on "language." Some possible categories could be "meaning makers," "hypothesis testers," "critical thinkers," and so on, if you should choose to structure the map. Guide the discussion of categories or terms in any way you prefer.

2. Discuss Gardner's theory of multiple intelligence. Focus on which facets are rewarded and ignored in a traditional class and how they can be developed through language arts.

3. Discuss the topic, "Many preschool reading programs are on the market today. Can reading occur without decentration?"

4. Discuss how the viewpoint "the young learner is a meaning seeker" differs from "the young learner is a sponge." How might your view of the young learner influence the way you teach?

5. Compare the home learning environment to a typical kindergarten environment in terms of how we know children acquire language.

STUDENT ACTIVITIES

1. Arrange for the students to visit a preschool. While they are there have them listen to the children's language for the following: 1) Are children talking to a teacher, another child, or themselves? 2) Do they carry on a conversation that goes beyond two or three consecutive interactions? Listen for the length of the communication unit. Assign a one-page summary of their observations, which includes a description of the context(s) in which the language occurred.

2. Tell the students to select preprimers from two sets of basal readers and analyze the language complexity as compared to language development of preschool children. Have them write a one-page paper on their findings.

3. Assign an article on language or thought development from an early childhood or child development journal. In two pages compare the journal ideas to those expressed in this chapter.

4. Tell the students to develop a classroom activity which clearly demonstrates the three levels of knowledge discussed in this chapter. (For example, draw a map showing how to get from home to school). They will share their activities in small groups.

5. The young child's sensitivity to rhythm and rhyme in oral language can be "a powerful springboard into literacy." Arrange for your students to visit (a) kindergarten classroom(s) at a time when they will most likely see a teacher using rhythm and/or rhyme activities to enhance a learning experience, in content other than music or movement. Assign a one-page paper, which includes a description of the activity, the students' behavior (including affect), and the teacher's behavior.

1. When a two-year-old refers to all round objects as "balls," his speech represents

    A. overextension of words.
    B. underextension of words.
    C. limited intelligence.
    D. phonemic analysis.

2. A child who accurately produces the stress shift in "photograph" and "photography" has applied his understanding of

    A. phonology.
    B. semantics.
    C. syntax.
    D. inflected endings.

3. The brain reaches 90% of its adult weight by age 5, mainly because

    A. the number of brain cells has increased.
    B. the size of the brain cells has increased.
    C. the interconnections among brain cells have increased.
    D. the size of the skull has increased.

4. The child who says "I *saw* a red bird" one week, then two weeks later states "I *see'd* a pretty butterfly" probably

    A. has regressed.
    B. is trying to apply a tacitly formulated rule.
    C. has limited intelligence.
    D. has delayed syntactic development.

5. Which is *not* given as a reason to examine the development of thought and language in children?

    A. You need to know what your children know.
    B. You need to know the ways children acquire language.
    C. You need to know children's common understandings or experiences.
    D. You need to facilitate organizing your children's classroom.

6. Which one of the following is *not* a separate intelligence?

    A. Musical
    B. Athletic
    C. Bodily-kinesthetic
    D. Logical-mathematical

7. Which is *not* an example of the patterns in development of language and thought?: going from

    A. listening to speaking.
    B. global to differentiated and integrated.
    C. universals to culture-specifics.
    D. the self to outside the self.

8. Uncle Ken and nephew Dave, both three years old, cannot agree whether Leo is father or grandfather. This is an example of difficulty with

   A. decentration.
   B. schema.
   C. concept attainment.
   D. metacognition.

9. Teaching children the strategies for working crossword puzzles is a form of

   A. decentration.
   B. metacognition.
   C. phonology.
   D. schemas.

10. If you apply the ideas of this chapter, language use in your classroom will be for

    A. talking.
    B. communicating.
    C. answering.
    D. singing.

11. Probably the most important factor for helping children develop good oral communication skills is good _____ skills.

    A. diagnostic
    B. organization
    C. modelling
    D. listening

12. A child's repetition of a song from a laxative commercial reflects

    A. the cultural background of the child.
    B. the child's sensitivity to rhythm and rhyme.
    C. the child's insensitivity to adult communication.
    D. a negative social context of language development.

13. The development of interconnections among brain cells

    A. usually is completed by age 11 or 12.
    B. cannot be influenced by teachers.
    C. results from learning.
    D. must be completed before learning can occur.

14. Before decentration, a child cannot do which of the following?

    A. Identify sounds of letters
    B. Identify names of letters
    C. Read a word in isolation
    D. Understand a story from the author's point of view

15. The utterance "Me go bye-bye" is an example of _____ language.

    A. babbling
    B. inflectional
    C. telegraphic
    D. metalinguistic

1. The child who knows how to change a declarative sentence to an interrogative sentence has a tacit command of

   A. phonology.
   B. semantics.
   C. syntax.
   D. structural analysis.

2. The development of the brain and the onset of language are

   A. random and determined by culture.
   B. sequential and not determined by culture.
   C. random and not determined by culture.
   D. sequential and determined by culture.

3. The cognitive difference between the average 7- to 8-year-old and the average 11- to 12-year-old is

   A. the younger cannot think abstractly.
   B. the older can think abstractly, but only when based on concrete experience.
   C. the younger cannot cognitively decenter.
   D. the older understands without having concrete experience of those relationships.

4. The statement "I go potty" represents

   A. functional speech.
   B. telegraphic speech.
   C. prosody.
   D. pragmatics.

5. When a child states "The blend is t-r" in response to a teacher's question, the child's statement reflects

   A. metalanguage.
   B. metacognition.
   C. prosody.
   D. pragmatics.

6. Which is *not* a brain characteristic?

   A. It absorbs like a sponge.
   B. It constructs perceptions and thought.
   C. It creates meaning.
   D. It anticipates.

7. A key ingredient of cognitive development is

   A. thinking about experiences.
   B. talking to peers.
   C. imitating parents.
   D. seeing relationships.

8. When students differentiate between "school" and "real" language, they most likely distinguish between

    A. reciting and communicating.
    B. "the king's English" and street dialect.
    C. formal grammar and peer language.
    D. regulatory and heuristic language.

9. If your classroom develops inquiring learners, you will use mostly _____ language.

    A. regulatory
    B. imaginative
    C. heuristic
    D. informative

10. "Me and John saw . . ." is an example of a _____ error.

    A. semantic
    B. syntax
    C. phonology
    D. schema

11. According to Bissex, a young child who "writes" (scribbles) a letter to Grandma and Grandpa represents the pattern

    A. acquisition of universals before culture-specifics.
    B. development from global to differentiated and integrated functioning.
    C. movement outward beyond the immediate in time and space and beyond our personal perspective.
    D. acquisition of culture-specifics before universals.

12. Children's first words represent

    A. words that parents teach them.
    B. a "universal" core of words that all children develop.
    C. things and people the children value.
    D. limited metalinguistic awareness.

13. If a young child makes the incomprehensible statement "I no gone wa-me" to an adult, the adult should

    A. realize the child is playing with the sounds of words.
    B. make the child repeat the statement until the meaning is clear.
    C. tell the child how well he is learning to talk.
    D. assume the child has something important to say.

14. The interaction of semantics, syntax, and phonology is determined by

    A. context and pragmatics.
    B. metacognition and context.
    C. context and content.
    D. content and pragmatics.

15. The degree to which the "communicative potential" of a child is realized is determined by

   A. other children.
   B. teachers.
   C. parents.
   D. all of the above.

3

Our Language Heritage

LECTURE DISCUSSION OUTLINE

THE DEVELOPMENT OF ORAL LANGUAGE

The Grand Ancestor: Indo-European

THE DEVELOPMENT OF WRITTEN LANGUAGE

THE ENGLISH LANGUAGE: A BRIEF HISTORY

Old English

Middle English

Modern English

American English

PROCESSES AFFECTING ENGLISH VOCABULARY

SUMMARY

The languages of half the earth's population can be traced to the Indo-European language, which existed approximately 7000 years ago somewhere in an area from the Balkans in eastern Europe to the Russian steppes north of the Black Sea. As speakers of Indo-European moved to other areas and lost contact with the original culture, their language changed. The English language grew from German, one of only nine languages to survive from the original Indo-European language. A basic understanding of the Indo-European language gives teachers insight into the structure of many languages and helps them assist students in their understanding of the origins and the vocabulary of a large number of words in English.

Written language began with the pictographic representations of prehistoric man. Gradually, logographic systems replaced pictures as the drawings became more stylized and represented one word or idea in a particular language. Eventually, the logographs came to represent sounds that were independent of their meaning, and then syllables. Syllabic writing had drawbacks, however, because so many symbols were needed and the reader had to have knowledge of what the text was probably about. The Greeks separated the consonants from the vowels and assigned symbols to each for an alphabetic system of writing. Knowledge of the sound equivalents for each of the letters enabled the reader to easily decode the message.

The history of the English language is divided into three periods: Old, Middle, and Modern English. Old English developed from the language spoken by the Germanic tribes—the Angles, Jutes, and Saxons—who invaded Britain around 410 A.D. The Anglo-Saxons contributed the core vocabulary of Modern English and many agricultural words. When monasteries were established around 600 A.D., Latin began to influence English, contributing many "church" terms. By the late eighth century, Danish vocabulary added considerably to Old English and improved its vocabulary, structure, and capacity to express meaning.

Middle English was most influenced by French, because that was the language of the court, parliament, and law. A large segment of French vocabulary was infused into the English language. Surnames emerged, a spelling standard developed, and the "Great Vowel Shift" occurred. By the end of the fifteenth century, the printing press was invented and the Renaissance's revival of Latin and Greek contributed many new words and spellings to English. By 1500, Middle English very closely resembled the English spoken today.

Modern English reflects the astounding advances in science and world exploration. Latin and Greek provided the building blocks for creating the new words needed for those advances. From 1558 to 1628 the language grew and changed at an unparalleled rate, especially from the contributions of William Shakespeare. By 1700 the stabilization of English spelling was almost complete.

American English was influenced by the European peoples who established settlements in the New World, the Native Americans, and the African/Americans. Spanish, Dutch, French, Native American, and the languages of western Africa all affected our language. The westward movement and immigration exerted strong influences on the development of American English during the nineteenth century. Immigrants from the Pacific Rim, Mexico, and Central and South America are still bringing more linguistic perspectives to our language today.

SUPPLEMENTARY DISCUSSION TOPICS

1. Disagreement exists today as to whether the printing press or the computer has had a more profound effect on mass communication. Discuss the issue with the whole class, focusing on how masses can read one book (the Bible) as one concept versus the production and distribution of so much information to so many people so quickly.

2. You might show several words from several languages that have common roots in Indo-European language and work with the concept of cognates.

3. Begin a discussion on how new words enter the language by sharing some words you have "invented." Have the students hypothesize about the meanings of the words and share how they arrived at them. In the discussion focus on new words from two separate words, from adding affixes to a root, from a foreign word, and so forth.

4. Discuss our spelling patterns, in light of the historical information presented here. Pay attention to the changes in the language, the ruling class, who controlled how a word was spelled, and similar issues.

5. Children use language to fit their world. They form new words and new expressions and alter the meanings of other words. This seems to be similar to what a whole culture does with its language. Discuss how teachers might view children's language versus communicating in the language of the school. Explore their feelings about slang and what happens if the teacher will communicate only in school language. (You might touch on accepting dialects for school communication or accepting "Spanglish".)

STUDENT ACTIVITIES

1. The invention of the alphabet may be the greatest technological advance in 2500 years. Debate the issue, "The invention of the alphabet contributed more to literacy than the printing press."

2. Teachers can use a resource file of word histories. From one of the sources listed at the end of this chapter have the students write a report on the etymology of a word of importance to them. During the sharing, each can start a bank of traced words.

3. Assign a two-page paper in which the student analyzes a language that is not Indo-European. Consider phonology, syntax, and semantics.

4. Have the students examine ten words from a list (basal reader, Dolch, spelling, and so on) and try to determine their origins. They can report either orally or in writing.

5. Have each student pick a culture and find ten words or expressions from it which have become a part of our language. Share in small groups.

6. Have each student find an American expression that has changed in meaning from when it was first introduced into the language. They can share those changes with the whole class.

7. Have each student find an American word that can be traced all the way back to its Indo-European roots. They can share their research and findings in small groups.

1. American English developed from which of the following languages?

   A. Anglo-Saxon
   B. British English
   C. Indo-European
   D. All of the above

2. A stylized drawing representing an idea in a particular language is _____ writing.

   A. pictographic
   B. logographic
   C. syllabic
   D. alphabetic

3. The Greeks developed an alphabetic writing system because

   A. they wanted a literate society.
   B. they wanted to spread their culture to other peoples.
   C. their language was syllabically too complex.
   D. their language contained too many words.

4. The capacity to express finer distinctions among concepts in Old English can be attributed to _____ vocabulary.

   A. Danish
   B. Anglo-Saxon
   C. French
   D. Spanish

5. Surnames emerged during which of the following periods?

   A. Old English
   B. Middle English
   C. Early Modern English
   D. Late Modern English

6. Shakespeare greatly influenced

   A. Old English.
   B. Middle English.
   C. Early Modern English.
   D. Late Modern English.

7. Noah Webster's desire to reform many English spellings reflects

   A. his strong sense of nationalism.
   B. his desire to make written communication easier.
   C. his desire to make spelling more "regular."
   D. none of the above.

8. The word "electrocardiograph" was formed by which of the following processes?

    A. Derivation
    B. Compounding
    C. Back formation
    D. Functional shift

9. Tracing word meanings through cognates takes advantage of

    A. meanings.
    B. spellings.
    C. dialect.
    D. both A and B.

10. In the long struggle to communicate in writing, which response is out of historical sequence?

    A. Represent experiences or the real world
    B. Syllabic representations
    C. Stylized symbols (cuneiforms)
    D. Alphabet

11. Which is *not* a period of English-language history?

    A. Old English
    B. Renaissance English
    C. Middle English
    D. Modern English

12. The *foundation* of Modern English comes from

    A. Celts.
    B. Romans.
    C. Angles, Jutes, and Saxons.
    D. Vikings.

13. In addition to professional scriveners producing more manuscripts than previously, they

    A. established a spelling standard.
    B. took religion out of manuscripts.
    C. invented the printing press.
    D. got rid of the French language.

14. According to the text, Shakespeare's contribution was that he

    A. could use Latin and Greek words.
    B. showed a need for dictionaries.
    C. established standardized spellings.
    D. combined various languages poetically.

15. That "American" English differs from "British" English is a natural extension of

    A. blending all the immigrants' languages.
    B. blending all the settlers' languages.
    C. absorbing native terms.
    D. all of the above.

1. A symbol representing a specific sound in a particular language is _____ writing.

    A. pictographic
    B. logographic
    C. syllabic
    D. alphabetic

2. Old English was most influenced by the

    A. Anglo-Saxons.
    B. Celts.
    C. French.
    D. Vikings.

3. Middle English was most influenced by the

    A. Anglo-Saxons.
    B. Celts.
    C. French.
    D. Vikings.

4. English during the Early Modern period

    A. changed very little.
    B. grew in compexity, but not in total number of words.
    C. was greatly influenced by French.
    D. grew and changed more than at any other time in history.

5. Which of the following statements about the influence of immigration on American English is most accurate?

    A. Immigration's influence was strongest during the nineteenth century.
    B. Immigration has played and continues to play an important role in its development.
    C. Immigration has influenced oral language, but not written language.
    D. Immigration has had little influence on American English.

6. An understanding of how our language has developed should help students

    A. view language as an ever-growing, ever-changing phenomenon.
    B. better understand themselves.
    C. develop more fully their communicative potential.
    D. all of the above.

7. The text's tracing diagram will help children follow a word

    A. over time.
    B. through different languages.
    C. as it evolves from one meaning to another.
    D. all of the above.

8. The Renaissance period brought a lot of silent letters to the English spellings, because scholars attempted to

   A. make the language more like Greek and Latin.
   B. reflect Greek and Latin origins of certain words.
   C. explain deep cultural and religious roots.
   D. communicate more easily with Rome.

9. It seems that affixes are used in the Modern English period to

   A. make the language as complex as Greek and Latin.
   B. simplify the contradictions between language influences.
   C. keep up with the explosion of knowledge at this time.
   D. make English sound like Latin and Greek.

10. Why might there have been no need for a spelling dictionary before the seventeenth century?

    A. Literacy was relatively uncommon.
    B. Because of all the influences, a standard spelling was not practical.
    C. The English language was changing too rapidly.
    D. English was not commonly used in business, law, and church.

11. Using "fridge" for "refrigerator" is a form of

    A. derivation.
    B. compounding.
    C. clipping.
    D. Functional shift.

12. Americans might not be as interested in Asiatic language roots, because English has _____ roots.

    A. Middle-Eastern
    B. Indo-European
    C. Northern European
    D. Southern European

13. Which of the following statements about the Middle English period can be attributed to the influence of the Renaissance?

    A. The spelling of many English words changed.
    B. The production of books increased.
    C. Universities were founded.
    D. Dictionaries were written.

14. Which did *not* influence Old English?

    A. Latin
    B. German
    C. Spanish
    D. French

15. Alphabetic writing simplified written communication by

    A. making the code system easier.
    B. making the letters easier to form.
    C. increasing the speed of communication.
    D. showing the need for the printing press.

4

Classroom Organization and Management

LECTURE DISCUSSION OUTLINE

SPECIAL CHARACTERISTICS OF CLASSROOMS THAT SUPPORT LEARNING

Risk taking

Talking

Integrated Instruction

ORGANIZING AND MANAGING THE PHYSICAL ENVIRONMENT

ORGANIZING AND MANAGING THE SOCIAL ENVIRONMENT

Classroom Procedures and Routines

    Transitions

Classroom Rules and Discipline

    A Range of Discipline Systems
    General Guidelines

Home and Community Involvement

ORGANIZING AND MANAGING THE ACADEMIC ENVIRONMENT

Goal Setting

Scheduling

Grouping

    Purposes of Grouping
    Role of Evaluation
    Forming Groups
        Special Interest Groups
        Cooperative Groups

Other Considerations

Thematic Units

Evaluating Learning

Involving Parents

SUMMARY

Risk-taking, freedom to talk, and integrated instruction characterize the integrated language arts classroom. Children and teachers need to feel free to make errors while learning and teaching, for learning occurs only when their mistakes are understood. Children must have confidence that peers or the teacher will not ridicule inaccurate responses, if they are to take the risks that foster learning. Talking is also essential to learning; students need to talk to teachers and to other students. Talk should be meaningful and focus on a present inquiry. Integrated instruction involves teaching and learning activities which include all the components of the language arts. Subject areas flow into each other and require longer blocks of time for learning and teaching.

A teacher has many options to physically arrange the classroom for effective instruction. Furnishings should be set up to accommodate different types of activities, to minimize problems with disruptive movement, and to facilitate monitoring of student work and behavior. There should be stable areas for the library, supply areas, art centers, and areas for turning in and storing student work in order for children to function independently. The teacher's desk and area for small group work should be located away from congested areas and placed so that all the students in the class can be observed. Student desks should be arranged to facilitate the type of instruction in which the students are engaged.

Classroom routines, rules, and discipline are concerns of all teachers. Because children are expected to internalize the rules and regulations of the classroom, once established, rules are difficult to change. Therefore, effective teachers decide on some basic rules before school begins and share them with the students very early in the first day of school. Other rules are added or revised through group discussion as situations arise. Classroom routines and procedures should be established early in the year. Students who know what to expect have more time for learning. Transitions should be carefully planned, because those times are when most problems occur. The type of discipline system a teacher chooses to use should be one that fits his or her personal philosophy and conforms to the school's guidelines. Systems range from very structured to less structured. Currently, Canter's *Assertive Discipline*, Gordon's *Teacher Effectiveness Training*, and Dreikurs' *Logical Consequences* are popular systems. Effective teachers try to prevent difficulties from occurring, however, by being aware of what is going on in the classroom, by being able to handle two situations at the same time, and by teaching well-paced, well-prepared lessons. Teachers effectively use parents, grandparents, and older students for working with small groups and providing individual attention.

Effective teachers set long-term and short-term goals for structuring the academic environment. They begin by formulating a brief yearly plan to establish the content that will be taught in each subject. Planning then becomes increasingly more detailed as teachers move to monthly, weekly, and daily plans. The current focus on literature-based reading has promoted the thematic approach to teaching. Planning for this approach is most easily accomplished when a group of teachers at the same level works together to develop units.

For efficiency of instruction, teachers group children in a variety of ways throughout the day. The size and make-up of groups are determined by the particular learning situation involved. The teacher's ongoing process of formal and informal evaluation of student academic ability and personal characteristics provides the information for grouping. In addition to groups formed for the teaching of a specific skill or ability level, interest groups and cooperative learning groups are used by effective teachers.

Evaluating students' work is a critical academic concern faced by all teachers. Each teacher must decide on a system that fits with the school policy on grading. In addition to report cards, effective teachers schedule parent conferences to inform parents about their child's progress.

SUPPLEMENTARY DISCUSSION TOPICS

1. Share and discuss some of the ideas from the cinquain poems that were written outside of class. (See student activity 1.)

2. This chapter contains several important concepts. Develop a semantic map on one of them and lead a discussion of the categories/attributes along whatever line you choose.

3. The physical arrangement of the classroom affects much of what happens in that room. Show transparencies of two or three classroom setups. Use the chapter ideas to guide the discussion about how each physical arrangement affects traffic flow, availability of books and supplies, communications, and so forth.

4. Discuss the three systems of discipline in this chapter in light of the open communication needed for integrated language arts. Which system(s) allow and/or encourage open communication and accepting personal responsibilities?

5. Discuss the contradictions in "portfolios for fourth graders." Call attention to "grading" as evaluating against a norm. On the other hand, the portfolio concept emphasizes growth from a point or skill.

6. It is a truism that good teachers take advantage of the moment and adjust to the immediate needs/interests of the learners. Lead a discussion on the apparent contradiction between this idea and the planning ideas expressed in this chapter. You might want to call attention to the need for planning to develop "integrated" language arts and to track language growth over time. Also, with goals firmly in mind, is the teacher better prepared to take advantage of those moments in a beneficial way?

STUDENT ACTIVITIES

1. Have each student write a cinquain poem on the chapter and share some in class, as your entry to a discussion. Your cinquain could follow this pattern:

    Main idea of chapter (one word)
    Synthesis of the parts (two words)
    Affective reaction to the author's ideas (three words)
    How the student will use the ideas in teaching (four words)
    Synonym (one word)
    See the sample from chapter 1, student activities #1.

2. Because this chapter has so many major concepts, you might break the class into small groups and let each map out one term. Discussing the terms from the map should help the students grasp the complexity and breadth of the issues.

3. Have the students plan and draw the physical arrangement of a classroom, which includes students' desks, teacher's desk, area for small group instruction, supply area, and library area. The plan should also include a written explanation of why they chose that particular arrangement. Have the students explain how they would modify their plan for state testing, cooperative-learning activities, and whole-class discussions.

4. Assign the students to explore appropriate curriculum guides for scope and sequence of the language arts skills for a grade level. Have them put together several language activities into a "unit," and in a one-page paper explain why they chose these activities and how much time they are allowing for this unit.

5. Assign a two-page paper about a time when the student was in charge of young people. Each student is to describe how s/he handled discipline and compare his/her system to those discussed in this chapter. You might want students to state why they would or would not do things differently, now that they are more knowledgeable about discipline.

6. Ask each student to interview a teacher about planning. Does the teacher have a year long, language arts plan? What are the differences between the weekly schedule of language arts activities and plans for teaching specific language skills? What are district requirements on planning? Building requirements? Students are to take notes on the interview and then discuss their findings in small groups.

7. To provide an easy experience with portfolio scoring, give each student a sample of primary-grade writing. In small groups have them list things that are right about the writing and skills that the child needs to work on. To introduce scope and sequencing, you might have them also try to sequence their lists from easier to more difficult skills.

1. A classroom that supports learning would feature

   A. children reading teacher comments in their journals.
   B. children seeking help from other children.
   C. children talking about how to spell a word.
   D. all of the above.

2. What is the most noticeable physical characteristic of an integrated language arts classroom?

   A. A variety of activities goes on at the same time.
   B. Students talk to each other a lot.
   C. The teacher encourages chatter in the classroom.
   D. Students work quietly on individual projects.

3. Which scene would *not* fit the integrated language arts classroom?

   A. Giving personal reports on a history topic
   B. An hour-long spelling period each day
   C. Children sharing dictated stories in the reading area
   D. Audience feedback to a reader's theater presentation

4. According to the text, in the language arts classroom supplies should be

   A. portioned carefully.
   B. distributed before lessons begin.
   C. freely available.
   D. under the direction of the helper.

5. Which statement is probably *not* true?

   A. *Assertive Discipline* depends on the teacher to solve the problems.
   B. *Teacher Effectiveness Training* relies on communication.
   C. *Logical Consequences* works because consequences are logical.
   D. A combination of all three systems is contradictory.

6. Which statement does *not* fit with the organization discussed in the text?

   A. Children asking to sharpen pencils
   B. Supplies freely available in a special location
   C. Special place for turning in completed work
   D. Special area for books and reading

7. Which is *not* a major concern for planning a thematic unit?

   A. Central content
   B. Dividing time
   C. Grading
   D. None of the above

8. In a supportive learning environment, the talk of several students enthusiastically discussing a recent slumber party while conducting a science experiment should be viewed

    A. positively because all talk is rewarded.
    B. negatively because the content of the talk is inappropriate.
    C. positively because the talk is meaningful to the students.
    D. negatively because students should not talk during an experiment.

9. To avoid classroom management problems during transitions, teachers might

    A. blink the lights to signal that an activity will soon end.
    B. encourage children to monitor the duration of their activities.
    C. have specific routines for collecting notes, turning in homework, and so on.
    D. all of the above.

10. Of the following, which aids discipline?

    A. "Withitness" and "overlapping"
    B. An environment with few rules
    C. Long transition times
    D. A "no talking" rule

11. One of the strengths of Canter's discipline system is that

    A. students solve the problems.
    B. material rewards increase intrinsic motivation.
    C. it is usually a school-wide program which results in consistency.
    D. children have a lot of input into the system.

12. The best way to find out why a child is misbehaving is to

    A. consult the principal.
    B. ask the parents.
    C. ask the child.
    D. consult the school psychologist.

13. Cooperative groups are popular today because they

    A. reduce competition.
    B. reduce individual accountability.
    C. stress individual goals.
    D. all of the above.

14. In order to be effective helpers in the classroom, parent volunteers need

    A. a high school diploma and at least one year of college.
    B. an understanding of the teacher's academic and behavioral expectations.
    C. a college degree.
    D. a basic understanding of teaching methodology.

15. Which is *not* a feature of an integrated language arts classroom?

    A. Three group rotations for fine-tuning skill lessons
    B. Large blocks of time for integrating contents
    C. Time allocated for assessment and teaching
    D. One hour set aside for the spelling lesson

EXAM 4-B

1. Which is *not* a feature of an integrated language arts classroom?

    A. The best papers displayed on a bulletin board
    B. Risk-taking in spelling on a composition
    C. Talking among the students
    D. Meaningful communication in more than one area of language arts

2. Which of the following scenes represents the special characteristics of a supportive learning environment?

    A. Several children discuss a play they are writing in a corner of the room.
    B. A child hypothesizes about how a story will end.
    C. Children write and illustrate a different ending to a story they have read.
    D. All of the above.

3. Which organization interferes with a free flow to the books?

    A. Materials available on a table near the center of the room
    B. Materials in bookcases around the room
    C. Materials in a case behind the reading instruction table
    D. Materials available in the school library

4. It is important to establish rules concerning which of the following?

    A. How many in a group working independently
    B. Forms of punishment
    C. What to do for early arrivals
    D. All of the above

5. The *best* way to handle discipline is

    A. prevent the situation from happening.
    B. firmly and without hesitation.
    C. gently and in a caring way.
    D. send the child to the principal.

6. Which is *not* a Callahan and Clark discipline suggestion?

    A. Expect mistakes.
    B. Anticipate negative behavior.
    C. Have fun with the students.
    D. Ignore some behaviors.

7. Which is *not* a use for grouping?

    A. Evaluation
    B. Special interests
    C. Competition
    D. Cooperative learning activities

8. A small group of students discussing the reasons why the colonists chose to declare independence from England demonstrates how

   A. special interest groups are formed.
   B. students use talk to refine concepts.
   C. teachers form groups for direct instruction.
   D. all of the above.

9. If you wanted to use the furniture in your classroom to facilitate a class meeting to discuss some recent problems on the playground, you would arrange desks

   A. in straight rows to prevent further discipline problems.
   B. in clusters of four to six to encourage small group discussion.
   C. in a large circle to increase student input.
   D. in two groups—one for the boys and one for the girls.

10. Supply areas in the classroom should be

    A. strictly controlled by the teacher.
    B. monitored by a student helper.
    C. *not* accessible to students who misbehave.
    D. easily accessible to all students.

11. Establishing routines

    A. creates a boring environment.
    B. frees children to focus on learning.
    C. is *not* appropriate in the integrated language arts classroom.
    D. should be done *after* discipline is under control.

12. If the discipline system a teacher has chosen is not working,

    A. the teacher has not implemented it properly.
    B. the system might not fit the personal philosophy of the teacher.
    C. the teacher should keep trying until it does work.
    D. the system needs more means of punishment.

13. Groups should be established

    A. for efficiency of instruction.
    B. for specific learning situations.
    C. by interest.
    D. all of the above.

14. Of the following statements, which is a true statement about parent volunteers?

    A. Parents should not work with small groups.
    B. Parents can help develop teaching units.
    C. Parents can help in and out of the classroom.
    D. Parents should maintain discipline so the teacher can teach.

15. Which one of the following is *not* a characteristic of cooperative grouping?

    A. Students learn how to balance individual accountability with group accountability.
    B. Students have different tasks for which they are responsible.
    C. Children will have different teachers for different content areas prior to attending middle school.
    D. Students are usually not as competitive.

The Teaching of Listening, Speaking, and Creative Dramatics

THE ROLE OF ORAL COMMUNICATION IN THE CLASSROOM

YOUR ROLE IN DEVELOPING ORAL COMMUNICATION SKILLS

Direct Teaching

> Modeling

Informal Learning Situations

> Demonstrating the Functions of Language

>> Instrumental
>> Regulatory
>> Interactional
>> Personal
>> Imaginative
>> Heuristic
>> Informative

LISTENING

Developing Skills from the Simple to the Complex

> Range of Instructional Situations
>> Natural and Created Sounds
>> Voices
>> Sequence
>> Anticipation
>> Critical Listening
> Examining Propaganda

Reading Aloud to Children

> Recommended Read-Aloud Books
> Directed Listening-Thinking Activity (DLTA)

Storytelling

SHARING AND ORAL PRESENTATIONS

Sharing

> Teacher-Directed Sharing
> Student-Directed Sharing

Oral Presentations

SMALL GROUP DISCUSSIONS

Getting Underway

Procedural Guidelines

The Teacher's Role in Small Group Discussions

CREATIVE DRAMATICS

Space and Organization

The "Basics" of Creative Dramatics

> Relaxation
> Concentration
> Trust
> Simple Movement
> "Quieting" Activities

From Fingerplays to People Plays

> Fingerplay
> Puppetry
> Pantomime
> Narrative Pantomime
> Children's Storytelling
> Improvisation
> Drama

SUMMARY

Oral communication is *the* foundation of classroom instruction, because speech is the bridge by which a child relates what is being taught to what s/he already knows. By developing oral communication skills, a teacher develops a child's potential to effectively learn reading, writing, and content-area skills. Through modeling, a teacher directly teaches how to communicate effectively. Informal learning situations involving one-to-one responses, or responses to a small group engaged in an activity, provide opportunities for indirect instruction. By taking time to "just talk" to students, by showing delight in the sounds and rhythms of words and phrases, or by responding to concerns or fears of students in a sensitive way, a teacher demonstrates effective communication and the various functions of language.

Effective oral communication depends not only on speaking but on good listening as well. Good listeners try to construct as closely as possible the intended message of the speaker. Success depends on the context of the situation and the listener's mood, interest, expectations, and knowledge. Listening skills should be developed from the simple to the complex. Directing children's attention to natural and created sounds and the quality of voices are simple activities that get children to attend to and respond to sound. More complex activities include sequence, developing anticipatory sets, and critical listening. The Directed Listening-Thinking Activity (DLTA) is an effective method for developing listening comprehension. Storytelling or daily reading aloud to children of all ages models the cadence and rhythm of the language of books and develops a child's sense of story. These activities not only motivate children to read, but also introduce them to the values and literary traditions of different cultures. The chapter contains guidelines for reading aloud, as well as extensive graded lists of recommended read-aloud books.

Sharing time (show-and-tell) is an excellent opportunity to develop the various functions of language. Both teacher-directed and student-directed sharing time can be effective, if students are taught how to deliver oral presentations and then given time to practice delivery. Small group discussions provide valuable opportunities to develop the critical thinking skills of systematically identifying issues or problems, defining their parts, and working through a problem-solving process to arrive at a conclusion. The reasoning done as a group becomes the foundation for independent problem solving. The chapter contains many examples and suggestions for teaching oral-language-production activities.

Creative dramatics link all the language arts in a type of symbolic expression that is easy for children to identify with and understand. It stimulates children's imagination and critical thinking, as well as helping them to understand themselves and the motivations underlying human behavior. Because it is such a powerful teaching tool, it should be a mainstay of the curriculum. The chapter contains a broad variety of dramatic activities, examples of each, and suggestions for incorporating them into the language arts program.

SUPPLEMENTARY DISCUSSION TOPICS

1. A long time observer of kindergarten show-and-tell activities states, "I see the teacher keeping the children in their space and asking the performer questions. Meanwhile, the child nods an answer, rather than communicating meaningfully with the audience." Discuss this situation in the light of "decentration."

2. Classrooms have a great diversity of students whose predominant language is other than English. With your students, examine personal feelings and knowledge of other languages and cultures. Explore their attitudes about teaching children from other cultures, and how they will teach oral communication skills to them.

3. Many people believe that watching television has little value in helping children acquire literacy. Discuss the values and limitations of children's programs in light of the ideas about oral communication expressed in this chapter. Prior to the discussion, have your students watch various types of children's television programs (cartoons, situation comedies, and special programs included).

4. Discuss how DLTA and small group discussions develop critical thinking skills.

5. In a whole-class discussion, apply Gardner's ideas of intelligence from Chapter 2 to the presentation on creative dramatics (especially critical thinking skills).

STUDENT ACTIVITIES

1. In small groups, have the students develop a checklist of things to look for while observing or sharing activities.

2. In small groups, have the students teach a DLTA. Each listener will participate in the lesson and then give feedback about both the content and process of the lesson.

3. Have students model oral reading of literature. The listeners will give feedback from a prepared list of skills.

4. In small groups or whole class, have the students brainstorm listening, oral language, and drama activities from a specific piece of literature.

5. In small groups, have the students prepare and tell a story, using the guidelines presented in this chapter. Out of the discussion that follows, develop a story telling file.

6. In small groups, let each student role-play leading a small group discussion, using the guidelines presented in this chapter. Participants will give feedback to the leader.

7. Assign readings in the literature about building trust, quieting activities, and relaxation techniques. Students can write a one-page paper on their findings or share them orally in small groups.

8. Have the students start a picture file or commercial script that exhibits the propaganda techniques presented in this chapter.

1. A group discussion of Charlotte's character traits (in *Charlotte's Web*) is an example of

    A. modeling oral communication.
    B. indirect instruction in oral communication.
    C. direct instruction in oral communication.
    D. testing oral communication.

2. A teacher might play animal sounds to

    A. teach vowel sounds.
    B. teach auditing.
    C. test hearing capacity.
    D. introduce young children to listening.

3. In the DLTA a child's prediction of what will happen next in the story is *not* based on

    A. picture information.
    B. story information.
    C. experiential information.
    D. knowing the story.

4. Because speaking/listening/reading/writing are interrelated in many ways,

    A. instruction in one area will almost always have an effect on the other areas.
    B. instruction should focus more on reading/writing than on speaking/listening.
    C. instruction should focus more on speaking/listening than on reading/writing.
    D. instruction in speaking/listening should be delayed until basic reading/writing skills are acquired.

5. Oral communication is the foundation for classroom instruction because it is

    A. easily taught.
    B. what the children already know.
    C. what the children need to know.
    D. difficult to teach.

6. A kindergarten teacher will teach about or use created sounds

    A. after voices.
    B. before natural sounds.
    C. after sequence.
    D. before voices.

7. When a popular athlete endorses a product in a commercial, it is a form of _____ language.

    A. personal
    B. informative
    C. regulatory
    D. interactional

8. The primary language function of propaganda is

   A. informational.
   B. heuristic.
   C. personal.
   D. regulatory.

9. To convince a person s/he is unique, is the *opposite* of

   A. plain folk and bandwagon.
   B. deck stacking and plain folk.
   C. name-calling and snob appeal.
   D. positive associations and testimonial.

10. An advertisement that says "Handy Wrap is twice as strong as before" is an example of

    A. testimonial propaganda.
    B. deck stacking propaganda.
    C. bandwagon propaganda.
    D. glittering generalities propaganda.

11. A child sharing a recent trip to the zoo is an example of

    A. object identification.
    B. performed narrative.
    C. lecture demonstration.
    D. object reporting.

12. The primary object for teaching _____ is cooperative and collaborative problem solving.

    A. narrative pantomime
    B. student-directed sharing
    C. oral presentations
    D. small group discussions

13. If a child in your class won't participate in creative dramatics, you will try _____ as an effective transition.

    A. mirror movement
    B. improvisation
    C. pantomime
    D. puppetry

14. Which of the following answer is *not* a basic of creative dramatics?

    A. Memorizing a few sentences
    B. Relaxation techniques
    C. Building trust
    D. Simple movement activities

15. Storytelling has become more popular in recent years because it

    A. takes little preparation.
    B. is a required part of the curriculum.
    C. introduces children to other cultures.
    D. teaches children to memorize.

1. Just talking to students during a science lesson is a form of

   A. direct teaching.
   B. direct testing.
   C. informal testing.
   D. informal teaching.

2. Listening to fill in a missing word or phrase represents

   A. anticipation.
   B. critical listening.
   C. DLTA.
   D. sequence.

3. Which statement does *not* describe the DLTA?

   A. It is more appropriate for upper elementary than primary students.
   B. It builds on what the child already knows.
   C. It is an effective teaching strategy for young children.
   D. It allows children to anticipate what might occur.

4. Oral language is taught as a means of communication and of

   A. testing.
   B. expression.
   C. teaching.
   D. learning.

5. The correct order for the text's continuum for developing listening skills from the simple to the complex is

   A. created sounds, natural sounds, sequence, voices.
   B. voices, created sounds, sequence, natural sounds.
   C. natural sounds, created sounds, voices, sequence.
   D. voices, natural sounds, created sounds, sequence.

6. The language most used and abused by teachers is

   A. instrumental.
   B. instructional.
   C. personal.
   D. regulatory.

7. "I want each of you in your seat!" is a form of _____ language.

   A. personal
   B. informal
   C. regulatory
   D. interactional

8. The statement, "Mary, many people are afraid of snakes. It's natural to be afraid of something that might hurt you" is an example of

   A. imaginative language.
   B. interactional language.
   C. heuristic language.
   D. personal language.

9. The beer commercials that show young, slender women wearing bathing suits in a vacation setting is a form of

   A. glittering generalities.
   B. bandwagon.
   C. testimonial.
   D. positive association.

10. A child sharing a favorite toy is an example of

    A. object identification.
    B. performed narrative.
    C. lecture demonstration.
    D. object reporting.

11. While leading a group reading lesson, your primary role is to

    A. maintain classroom discipline.
    B. facilitate the group discussion process.
    C. summarize each group's results.
    D. assign the topic.

12. The rudiments of improvisation are learned through

    A. movement activities and narrative pantomime.
    B. puppetry and narrative pantomime.
    C. movement activities and puppetry.
    D. puppetry and finger plays.

13. Speech bridges the learning to

    A. previous experiences.
    B. the unknown.
    C. the teacher.
    D. none of the above.

14. Creative dramatics should be used to

    A. stimulate the imagination.
    B. stimulate critical thinking.
    C. increase understanding of oneself.
    D. all of the above.

15. The "heart" of creative dramatics is

    A. memorizing.
    B. play.
    C. movement.
    D. entertainment.

6

The Processes and Development
of Reading and Writing

LECTURE DISCUSSION OUTLINE

WHAT IS TO BE LEARNED: THE NATURE OF WRITTEN LANGUAGE

The Purposes of Written Language

The Content and Form of Written Language

    Narrative Structure
    Expository Structure

THE PROCESSES OF WRITING AND READING

The Process of Writing

The Process of Reading

    The Interactive Nature of The Reading Process
    Components of The Reading Process

THE DEVELOPMENT OF READING AND WRITING

The Preschool Years: Birth Through Kindergarten

    Reading
        Reading to Children
    Writing
        Scribbles and Drawing
        Approaching Alphabetic Writing

The Primary School Years: First Through Third Grade

    Beginning Conventional Literacy and the Development of Word Knowledge
        Children's Reading
        Children's Writing
        Development of Word Knowledge in Reading and Writing

Transitional Reading and Writing
    Children's Reading
    Children's Writing and Spelling

The Intermediate School Years: Fourth Through Sixth Grade

    Background Knowledge or Content Schemata
    Knowledge of Genre Schemes or Text Schemas
    Knowledge of the Information Encoded in Writing Itself

SUMMARY

The purposes or functions of written language are the same as those of oral language. Only the terms used to describe the purposes—poetry, narrative, description, exposition, and persuasion—are different. The writer's purpose determines the form and content of written expression. Form and content have a reciprocal relationship in that each influences the other: the content determines the genre scheme selected by the author; the genre scheme influences how the author organizes and expresses the content.

To facilitate learning one must understand how the processes of reading and writing are both similar and different. For both activities, individuals must draw upon background knowledge, knowledge of syntax, genre schemes, and the information encoded in writing. In addition they must have the prerequisite understandings about the nature of reading/writing and the conventions of writing and print. Although the specific skills involved in reading and writing differ, to be efficient in either, lower-level aspects must be automated to allow more processing time, cognitive space, and energy for higher-level aspects. While engaged in reading or writing, an individual must "balance" automated and conscious functions. In addition, both reading and writing are learned in social contexts. A general uniformity exists in what young children know about reading and print and how they acquire that knowledge. Differences in levels of literacy among children stem from how they apply that knowledge.

Literacy development begins during the preschool years. During that time, through processes of increasing integration and differentiation, young children develop many concepts about reading and writing. They know that writing is separate from pictures and is meant to convey information. They develop a basic understanding of "story," "book," directionality in reading and writing, and how alphabetic characters are used and combined. They are aware that the language of books is different from normal conversation.

Formal reading instruction begins with the development of simple "story grammars," a sight vocabulary, and strategies for word identification. As lower-level word identification becomes automated, fluency increases and reading comprehension comes more in line with listening comprehension. During the intermediate grades, instruction focuses on helping students apply their ever-expanding background knowledge as they read new text. In addition instruction focuses on developing students' knowledge of more elaborate text schematas (especially those of expository text) and structural analysis.

Formal writing instruction parallels reading instruction. During the primary years writing instruction should focus on helping children become comfortable with expressing thoughts through writing and then guiding them along the developmental process. It is essential that the writing efforts of young children be accepted and praised. Most of their energy and cognitive space must be devoted to letter formation and encoding. The use of invented spelling should be encouraged not only because it helps "free" children to communicate ideas, but also because it ultimately contributes to growth in spelling. Initially, children's writing is egocentric and of a personal nature. With practice and increased reading knowledge, it progresses to poetic and transactional voices. As lower-level skills are automated, more attention can be focused on content. The length of writing increases, and they incorporate conventions of style and mechanics in their writing. During the intermediate grades, students experiment with different forms of writing and types of elaboration. They gain control of their writing and are able to read their writing as another person would read it, which contributes to their revising and editing skills. By the end of the intermediate years writing can be a craft but also has the potential to be a very significant tool for both learning and personal growth.

SUPPLEMENTARY DISCUSSION TOPICS

1. Because some teachers have difficulty making distinctions between teacher assignment writing and student, meaningful, communicative writing, you might brainstorm ideas for writing topics with the students. Then group the entries into two categories: for writer's purpose and for teacher's purpose, and discuss why each entry fits its category.

2. Conduct a reading or a writing lesson in a nonstandard alphabet. Focus on the students' feelings and processes. Then relate this experience to how a child must feel in beginning reading/writing lessons and what the implications are for teaching them.

3. Role-play a parent-conference situation where the teacher believes in integrated reading and writing techniques and the parent is upset about invented spelling, grammatical errors, and so forth, on the papers coming home. Choose one student to play the role of the teacher. Choose another to play the parent role. You might also have a "principal" or curriculum person sit in to help the teacher.

4. Integrated language arts speaks to accepting children where they are, rather than having them fit into the school curriculum for reading and writing. Discuss the teaching difficulties of preparing an experience that taps into all the "knowledges" the diverse learners bring from their backgrounds.

STUDENT ACTIVITIES

1. Have the students develop a cinquain poem on the contents of the chapter, as described in student activities from earlier chapters. They might share their poems in small groups.

2. Have the students search the professional literature for an article on a code-based approach to teaching reading. Write a two-page paper on the points of that approach and compare it to the integrated language arts approach.

3. Have the students observe in a preschool/kindergarten class for a period of time and record/describe the various ways the children are exposed to print. Include labels for objects, name tags, LEA activities, and other ways.

4. Have the students observe in a preschool/kindergarten class for a period of time and record/describe the various ways the children attempt to write or read. Include any evidence of global writing activities and attempts to communicate thoughts or experiences in some coded message. They can also include activities that show "reading" by reciting memorized texts.

5. Have the students observe in a primary class for a period of time and record/describe the various ways the children use invented spelling, meaningful communication, student purpose for writing, and so on. Students should note the teacher's acceptance, encouragement, and/or reaction to these aspects when they happen.

6. Have the students interview a classroom teacher about the school/district policy on invented spelling, developmental writing skills, and the reading/writing connection. They can write a two-page summary of the interview, including their own reactions.

7. Have the students obtain district literacy statements (possibly from curriculum guides or school handbooks). In a two-page paper, have them compare the district statements with the ideas in this chapter on literacy.

1. The relationship between the form and content of written expression is best described as

   A. contrapuntal.
   B. developmental.
   C. reciprocal.
   D. sequential.

2. A paper explaining photosynthesis is an example of which type of informational writing?

   A. Persuasive
   B. Expressive
   C. Expository
   D. Descriptive

3. Because reading and writing are complex processes,

   A. specific skills are difficult to teach.
   B. consciously attending to all aspects is impossible.
   C. automation of skills is difficult.
   D. each must be mastered before integrating instruction.

4. Written expression is most controlled by

   A. genre schemes.
   B. content.
   C. author's purpose.
   D. verbal efficiency.

5. If a preschool child can identify "Oreo," "milk," and "Jello," when shopping at a grocery store, you can assume the child

   A. knows the letters of the alphabet.
   B. has associated a printed symbol with an object or action.
   C. knows how to read.
   D. has figured out letter/sound relationships.

6. A young child who "reads" a book by reciting the story from memory, while turning the pages and pointing to print, is one who has

   A. a basic concept of story.
   B. been read to.
   C. a concept of directionality.
   D. all of the above.

7. The acquisition of a sight vocabulary is

   A. essential to beginning readers.
   B. essential for spelling.
   C. the product of letter/sound teaching.
   D. not required until the end of the first grade.

8. "MKT LKM" ("My cat likes me") represents which stage of spelling development?

   A. Semiphonemic
   B. Letter-name
   C. Within-word pattern
   D. Logographic

9. Children are able to make fuller use of writing in an "epistemic" manner during

   A. the preschool years.
   B. first grade.
   C. second and third grades.
   D. fourth through sixth grades.

10. Reading efficiency depends upon a reader's knowledge of

    A. the topic.
    B. the text schema.
    C. word structure.
    D. all of the above.

11. With which instructional practice would the text agree?

    A. Encouraging primary students to use invented spelling
    B. Requiring third graders to use the dictionary for all unknown words
    C. Encouraging first graders to write a ten-sentence story
    D. Telling intermediate students to focus on spelling during the first draft

12. With which instructional practice would the text agree?

    A. Encouraging intermediate students to use narrative reading strategies when reading content materials
    B. Teaching students organizational patterns of expository texts
    C. Cautioning students not to use background knowledge when reading
    D. All of the above

13. Children's invented spelling should

    A. be discouraged.
    B. be helpful to teachers in pinpointing instruction.
    C. be accepted, but later corrected.
    D. be used to generate weekly spelling words.

14. Which do the children *not* draw on as they read and write?

    A. Knowledge of text schemas
    B. Knowledge of syntax
    C. Modality knowledge
    D. Background knowledge

15. To which of the following are students most likely to attend during expository writing?

    A. Characterization
    B. Cause/effect relationship
    C. Conflict
    D. Setting

1. Genre schemes

    A. influence how authors organize and express content.
    B. determine the author's purpose.
    C. determine the content of written expression.
    D. all of the above.

2. Which represents persuasive writing?

    A. A paper explaining symbiosis
    B. A position paper on arms reduction
    C. An article describing the aftermath of an earthquake
    D. A play about the California gold rush

3. Reading is _____ process.

    A. a cognitive
    B. a complex
    C. an interactive
    D. all of the above

4. Children in first and second grade generally do not produce well-developed written stories because

    A. they have not been taught how to "make up" stories.
    B. they lack the required experiential background.
    C. they do not have the knowledge about print or the processing time that allows for higher-level aspects.
    D. teachers do not expect well-developed stories.

5. When adults direct children's attention to environmental print, they are

    A. teaching children to read.
    B. helping children become aware of the form and function of print.
    C. developing the child's vocabulary.
    D. all of the above.

6. The concept of word in print is

    A. learned during the preschool years.
    B. essential to reading.
    C. more important for spelling than for reading.
    D. all of the above.

7. During the transitional stage, reading is

    A. fairly fluent and done silently.
    B. fluent but still needs a lot of guided support.
    C. characterized by increased reasoning power.
    D. slow because word identification is not automated.

8. Writing and reading primarily become tools for self-expression and learning

   A. in the first grade.
   B. during the second or third grade.
   C. during the fourth through sixth grade.
   D. after the sixth grade.

9. Word knowledge growth

   A. occurs steadily throughout the elementary years.
   B. is greatest during the primary years.
   C. is greatest during the transitional stage.
   D. is greatest during the intermediate years.

10. Which is probably the most important print source for developing literacy?

    A. The label on "Oreo" cookies
    B. A "stop" sign
    C. *The San Francisco Chronicle*
    D. *The Gingerbread Man*

11. The text views reading as a

    A. product of the text and reader.
    B. process of interaction between text and reader.
    C. product of the author and reader.
    D. process of interaction between author and text.

12. With which instructional practice would the text agree?

    A. Discourage first graders from using a finger for tracking
    B. Encourage third graders to "whisper" as they read silently
    C. Encourage intermediate students to monitor their reading
    D. Discourage the use of sight words by first grade students

13. With which instructional practice would the text agree?

    A. Encourage primary students to use invented spelling
    B. Teach intermediate students organizational patterns used in expository texts
    C. Encourage the use of background knowledge for reading
    D. All of the above

14. A child's writing "The aligaiter went into the enormmous lake" represents

    A. semiphonemic spelling.
    B. letter-name.
    C. the within-word pattern stage.
    D. the logographic stage.

15. Which features of our language base are common to both reading and writing?

    A. Syntax
    B. Schemata
    C. Word knowledge
    D. All of the above

7

The Teaching of Writing

LECTURE DISCUSSION OUTLINE

FRAMEWORK FOR THE TEACHER: HOW CAN WRITING BE TAUGHT EFFECTIVELY?

"Natural" or "Structured" Process?

> Conferencing
> Direct Teaching
> Modeling
> Textbooks and Prepared Materials

THE WRITING PROCESS: PUTTING UNDERSTANDING INTO PRACTICE

Components of the Writing Process

> Prewriting
> Drafting
> Revising
> Editing
> Sharing and Publishing

Helping Young Children Become Comfortable with Writing

Teaching, Modeling, and Applying the Writing Process

> Using Conferences in Writing Instruction
> > Questioning in Teacher/Student Conferences
> > Questioning in Student/Student Conferences
> Prewriting
> > Drawing
> > Clustering
> > Brainstorming
> > Stream-of-Consciousness Writing
> Drafting
> Revising

SUMMARY

Children learn to write by writing. Effective teaching of writing includes both "natural" and "structured" process writing. In addition, the environment and the context of situation must be supportive and appropriate. Students need to write frequently and for different purposes, so that all stages of the writing process are addressed. Through conferencing or small response groups, students' writing and thinking can be refined. Teachers must provide direct instruction of skills. Sometimes this will occur when the students need it. Sometimes it is done when the teacher believes it is best. Teachers, however, must balance efficiency of instruction with maintaining the student's initiative and authority as a writer. Modeling the process of writing is a very effective method to show students that anyone can write, and takes the mystique out of writing. Although they are often not based on student-generated writing, textbooks and other prepared materials can be beneficial when used in a supportive way.

The teaching of writing has undergone significant changes in the past few years. No longer based on an English textbook, it is taught as a process involving prewriting, drafting or composing, revising, editing, and sharing or publication. The purpose of prewriting is to get thoughts and ideas going and then written down. Drawing, clustering, brainstorming, and stream-of-consciousness writing are effective prewriting activities. Students also begin to consider what they want their audience to gain from reading their composition. Most of the actual writing occurs during the drafting stage. Expressing meaning and intent are foremost on the writer's mind; they are generally developed through internal conversation. After the first draft comes the revision stage. Elaboration, clarification, deletion, or reordering of ideas are done to make the purposes or intentions of the writer more precise. A clear understanding of purpose is essential at this stage. During the editing stage the writer attends to spelling, grammar, and punctuation, as s/he prepares the composition for sharing or publication. Knowing a composition will be shared publicly gives a worthwhile purpose for editing. The sharing or publishing stage is essential to the writing process because the excitement students experience when others appreciate their work motivates further writing, which leads to increased growth in writing.

Writing is a tool to be used across the curriculum. Beyond expository writing, which was presented in the chapter, children can use a "writing log" in science or social science, create word problems in math, and so forth. The final topic is using the computer as a tool for writing. Limited research seems to show that keyboarding does not necessarily improve communication skills over the "hunt and peck" method. Word processing on microcomputers makes children's revising and editing work easier than with pen and pencil and appears to motivate them to write more. Pen and pencil, however, will never be completely replaced!

SUPPLEMENTARY DISCUSSION TOPICS

1. With the whole class (or in small groups) develop (a) semantic map(s) on the concept of writing.

2. By this time your students may be very involved with writing a cinquain, if they wrote one for the first several chapters. Sharing and discussing their ideas can also be quite informative.

3. Teachers are generally reluctant to send home writing work that is less than perfect. Explore your students' feelings about holistic evaluation of writing and publishing works that accurately reflect the children's skills. You might also delve into how the students will deal with those feelings.

4. So often teachers rely on textbooks or out-of-group experiences as the springboard for discussion, rather than use group experiences to deal with the same concepts or skills. For example, in a mixed ethnic group the children may read a story about prejudice, but not write about their feelings or the situation when they are called names on the school playground. This chapter serves as a great springboard to talk about having children write about common (everyday) experiences.

STUDENT ACTIVITIES

1. Find classrooms where process writing is used. Have the students observe and write a two-page paper describing the procedures they observed, such as brainstorming, drafting, peer feedback, revising, and publishing. They might include personal reactions to the process and evaluation statements about how it appears to be working.

2. Find classrooms where teachers use journals as a part of the writing program. Have your students observe the activities and in a two-page paper describe what the teacher and children are doing.

3. Have your students observe in a classroom for all the ways the children share or publish their work. Then your students might interview the teacher to get more ideas about how s/he publishes children's work, beyond what was observed. Your students could enter the ways in a data base, to be shared with all the classmates.

4. Have the students write a cinquain poem on the content of chapter 7. Follow or modify the form that was presented in earlier chapters.

5. Have your students observe in a classroom for a period of time and identify different classroom situations which could serve as topics for "log" writing. "Johnny's" classroom misbehavior might have all the elements of a story about some adult, non-socially acceptable act. Enter the lists in a data base for sharing with all the students.

6. Have your students examine curriculum materials and list topics that might lend themselves to writing in different areas of the curriculum. They can enter these ideas in a data base to be shared with all the other students. In small groups they could also share their lists and explain how they could be used.

1. Which is *not* a form of transactional writing?

   A. Poetry
   B. Description
   C. Exposition
   D. Persuasion

2. Which is a form of sharing?

   A. Interactions during teacher evaluation time
   B. Conferencing with classmates
   C. Posting writing on a bulletin board
   D. All of the above

3. If the Bay Area Writing Project focuses writing instruction on the process, probably its greatest impact is that children

   A. get more time to improve their communication skills.
   B. work through authoring stages to develop each piece.
   C. focus as much on the content of communication as the form.
   D. produce a finished product more quickly.

4. The teacher who has the children write at the beginning of the day, while taking attendance and lunch count, most likely skips which step in this activity?

   A. Prewriting
   B. Sharing
   C. Peer feedback
   D. Publishing

5. Which probably does *not* fit with "natural" writing?

   A. Writing about what is of interest to students
   B. Revisions based on a skill lesson about sentence combining
   C. Getting and giving peer feedback
   D. Revisions based on interactions with peers

6. Which is *not* a stage of writing development?

   A. Alphabetic
   B. Egocentric
   C. Audience-awareness
   D. Personal growth

7. Which is *not* an appropriate "prewriting" activity for the teacher?

   A. Web ideas on a topic with the group.
   B. Brainstorm sensory words with the class.
   C. Present an assigned topic to the class.
   D. Present an example of the assigned topic from the literature.

8. Which is *not* an appropriate "revision" activity?

   A. Reordering the thoughts
   B. Expanding on an idea
   C. Sentence combining/expansion
   D. Improving penmanship

9. Which is *not* a function of "editing"?

   A. Spelling
   B. Grammar
   C. Punctuation
   D. Brainstorming

10. Including a child's poem in the PTA announcement to all homes is a form of

    A. editing.
    B. revising.
    C. publishing.
    D. none of the above.

11. Writing a piece that tries to get others to agree with you about a point or process is _____ writing.

    A. descriptive
    B. persuasive
    C. poetry
    D. exposition

12. Possibly the most important aspect of natural writing is the development of

    A. better spelling and grammar skills.
    B. longer compositions.
    C. greater interest in writing.
    D. improved sense of audience.

13. Which is *not* true about English textbooks and other prepared materials?

    A. They are not usually based on students' writing.
    B. They should play a supportive role in your writing program.
    C. They should be the foundation of your writing program.
    D. They provide well-structured reinforcement.

14. Interactions with the teacher and peers during the drafting stage

    A. facilitate the development of internal conversation.
    B. aid in correcting punctuation and grammar.
    C. facilitate topic selection.
    D. all of the above.

15. Which is *not* usually addressed in primary grade writing?

    A. Characterization
    B. Setting
    C. Conflict
    D. Theme

1. Which is *not* a step in transactional writing?

    A. Use the student as the "expert."
    B. Web.
    C. Use interviews to get informed information.
    D. Use print to get informed information.

2. Which sharing step is *not* in sequence?

    A. Student reads his/her composition.
    B. Respond and ask probing or clarification questions.
    C. Focus on what the writer can do with the composition.
    D. Ask probing questions about the content.

3. If the Bay Area Writing Project focuses on writing as communication, probably its greatest impact is that children

    A. play a central role in improving their own writing skills.
    B. write better for other children than for teachers.
    C. are better helpers than teachers.
    D. like to communicate more than they did years ago.

4. The teacher who conducts one-day writing activities and then has the children revise for spelling, grammar, and penmanship, most likely skips which step?

    A. Prewriting
    B. Peer feedback
    C. Sharing
    D. Publishing

5. Which is *not* true about published writing activities?

    A. Readily available
    B. Based on children's writing
    C. Need little planning by the teacher
    D. Play a supportive role for your program

6. During the "drafting" stage, on which should the writer *not* focus?

    A. Meaning and intent
    B. Audience and voice
    C. Spelling and punctuation
    D. Hearing his/her inner voice

7. Which of the following illustrates ways to share students' compositions?

    A. The "Author's Chair"
    B. A school newspaper
    C. Books to be catalogued and placed in the library
    D. All of the above

8. Which is *not* a step in direct teaching of writing?

   A. Group brainstorms on a topic.
   B. Teacher models a writing skill.
   C. Children practice on an assignment.
   D. Children transfer the skill to other writing.

9. Which category is *not* a part of teacher/student conferences?

   A. Expanding and elaborating
   B. Refining sentences, word choice, and phrasing
   C. Correcting form problems
   D. Helping students see their own development as writers

10. Which is *not* a primary attribute of "structured" writing?

   A. Interaction with peers
   B. Teacher selection of materials and activities
   C. Primarily focused on writing of narratives
   D. Activities modeled by the teacher

11. Which activity would help a fifth grade student overcome a tendency to be overly concerned about spelling and word choice during prewriting?

   A. Clustering
   B. Brainstorming
   C. Stream-of-consciousness writing
   D. Drawing

12. During the revision stage, a writer

   A. should focus on correcting spelling and punctuation.
   B. needs to rewrite his composition.
   C. should not request peer feedback.
   D. must have a clear understanding of purpose.

13. Interest in editing is developed when students

   A. who find the most mistakes are rewarded.
   B. are punished for not finding errors.
   C. are not required to edit every composition.
   D. know their work will be published.

14. Which sequence represents the three-step process for teaching expository writing?

   A. Printed sources, interviews, student as "expert"
   B. Student as "expert," interviews, printed sources
   C. Interviews, printed sources, student as "expert"
   D. Student as "expert," printed sources, interviews

15. The text would *not* agree with which statement about microcomputers?

   A. Computer instruction should begin with keyboarding.
   B. Computers motivate children to write.
   C. Children can do simple word processing.
   D. Even limited computer time can be beneficial to students.

8

The Teaching of Reading

LECTURE DISCUSSION OUTLINE

READING INSTRUCTION WITHIN AN INTEGRATED LANGUAGE ARTS PROGRAM

Direct Teaching

    Modeling

Conferencing

Textbooks and Published Materials

BEGINNING READING

"Predictable" Texts

The Language Experience Approach

    Group Experience Charts
    Individual Dictations

Word Banks

IDENTIFYING WORDS

Whole Words

Word Analysis

    Phonics
    Structural Analysis
        Syllabication
        Prefixes, Suffixes, Base Words, and Word Roots
    Context Clues

SUMMARY

Because children learn to read by reading, developing students' desire to read is of primary importance. Reading and reading instruction must occur in meaningful contexts and must be enjoyable. Students need to see teachers engaged in meaningful reading, not only through read alouds, but also during sustained silent reading (SSR). Direct instruction of skills through modeling and teacher/student conferences are effective ways to teach reading. Time for free reading (usually through SSR) and oral reading are important elements of the total reading program. Too often all the time spent on reading is devoted to "instruction" and children never have time for "real reading." Oral reading should be used to check comprehension, to enhance appreciation of different genres, and to assess and evaluate reading development.

Historically basal reading series have been the foundation for reading instruction in the United States. Their underlying philosophy was that if skills are taught in a certain sequence, students will become readers. Current research refutes this concept, however. Reading is *not* the product of students' mastery of a specified sequence of isolated skills. During the past decade, many basal series incorporated such insights about the reading process. Nevertheless, some educators still argued against the use of any basal reading program, and quite recently publishers have begun to introduce new reading series based on the content and techniques of literature-based reading. Both "traditional basals" and "literature-based" reading series can be effective if used flexibly and as *part* of a total reading program. Good basal programs provide the following:

1) scope and sequence in comprehension and word study that more closely match the developmental competencies of students; 2) lesson formats for direct teaching of important skills; 3) types and sequences of questions that facilitate reading comprehension; 4) suggested related readings to accompany selections in the basals.

Beginning reading should occur in a natural context that gradually moves children from an experiential to an analytical perspective. Children must also develop concepts about the whole reading process before they are taught the pieces. Predictable texts and language experience approaches (LEA) are excellent ways to begin reading instruction for both kindergarten and first grade children who have the prerequisite understandings and information about print. Predictable texts, including the currently popular Big Books, provide the support beginning readers need because children can anticipate the language and story. Beginners rely heavily on memory for text. The LEA uses the language and experiences of children. Through group-dictated experience charts and individual dictations, children come to understand the features and functions of written language in a very natural way. The chapter includes a detailed explanation of the three-day cycle and how word banks can be used for skills instruction.

Development in reading requires mastery of word identification. Students first must learn to recognize whole words, and then learn word analysis skills. Knowledge of phoneme/grapheme correspondence facilitates growth in reading at the primary levels. At the intermediate grade levels examining structural or morphemic elements as part of structural analysis or vocabulary study is important. Instruction in comprehension should focus on developing vocabulary, identifying relevant information in texts and understanding how this information is related, knowing which reading strategy to use with the text, and responding to the information. The type of text, narrative or expository, and the reader's purpose for reading determine which strategies the reader should use for optimal comprehension. For narrative texts the Directed Reading-Thinking Activity (DRTA), story maps, and focusing on specific elements in a story are effective methods for developing comprehension. The DRTA teaches students to combine their prior knowledge with information in the text to predict, confirm, or revise predictions and develop their critical thinking skills. Students take the active role reading requires. A detailed explanation of the DRTA process is included in the chapter. Story maps help teachers develop pertinent questions and graphically show students the significant elements of narratives. When students have a lot of experience with narratives, focusing on specific elements helps them appreciate how writers develop characters and plots. They can then apply that understanding to their own writing. The content DRTA, the Prereading Plan, reading "road maps," interactive reading guides, and outlining are effective methods to help students organize, retain, and recall information presented in expository texts. An integral part of teaching these strategies is teaching students the various ways expository texts in different contents are organized.

Questioning and understanding the nature of questions are key components in facilitating comprehension and critical thinking. Teachers must work on their own questioning techniques and also help students understand the various levels of questions and the information required to answer them. Students' metacognition of questions can be developed effectively through instruction in Question Answer Relationships. The chapter describes this process in detail.

SUPPLEMENTARY DISCUSSION TOPICS

1. Do a semantic map on any of the major topics from this chapter (such as DRTA, LEA, and Big Books), or on the main topic, READING. Students' responses should lead to some lively discussions.

2. Debate the issue, "The DRA is as good for developing comprehension skills as the DRTA."

3. Openly discuss feelings/attitudes about a skills approach to reading versus an integrated language arts approach.

4. Discuss the difference between how teachers generally organize for language instruction (grouped children moving through a set continuum of skills) versus what we know about how children acquire language skills.

5. Compare and contrast the assumptions and procedures of a basal approach to reading versus a language experience approach versus a literature-based approach. Often a graphic post-organizer can be developed from this activity.

6. Distribute samples of children's dictated stories from experiences. Have your students compare experience content, sentence patterns, and vocabulary load with a traditional preprimer and/or primer of a basal reading series.

STUDENT ACTIVITIES

1. Have the students pick five Big Books and analyze their contents for literary value (character, setting, conflict, and theme).

2. Distribute samples of children's stories dictated from experiences. Be certain that you have three or four stories from the same child. Have the students analyze the sentences for complexity of patterns and vocabulary difficulty.

3. Have your students observe in a classroom where the children regularly get time for sustained silent reading. In a two-page paper they can describe the children's procedures for reading, exchanging books, and moving around the room. Also have them describe what the teacher does while the children read.

4. Have your students check with parents, where appropriate, and find out what the students' first favorite words were. Then have students try to figure out when they would have encountered them in a basal program. Similarly, they can figure out when they used the generally accepted ten most common ones.

5. Assign a two-page paper in which the student reads an article by a skills-oriented person and compares that point of view with that of the text.

6. Have your students observe in a classroom where the teacher uses a literature-based approach to beginning reading instruction (including the Big Books). In a two-page paper they can describe some of the teacher's and children's

activities related to the books. Also have them describe, if they can, the feelings and attitudes of the children toward reading in this approach.

7. Have your students observe in a classroom where the teacher uses DRTA in the reading program. In a two-page paper let them describe the kinds of questions the children ask, the procedures the teacher uses (picture, title, story clues before the reading), and the participation by the children.

1. An effective reading program teaches reading

    A. in meaningful content.
    B. in reading strategies.
    C. in meaningful context.
    D. all of the above.

2. Which is *not* a part of the reading conference?

    A. Sharing
    B. Oral reading
    C. Records keeping
    D. Testing

3. Which is *not* true about traditional basal readers of the past?

    A. Product-oriented
    B. Highly stimulating
    C. Uniformity and control
    D. Behavioristic model

4. Prerequisite experiences about reading include

    A. directionality.
    B. writing stands for speech.
    C. concept of story.
    D. all of the above.

5. Which is *not* a part of the group experience chart?

    A. Teacher pronounces the written words.
    B. Teacher emphasizes letter formation.
    C. Teacher preserves children's actual language.
    D. Teacher models top-to-bottom progression.

6. Big Book activities do *not* include

    A. pointing to words as read.
    B. filling in the missing word from context clues.
    C. teaching how to confirm a prediction.
    D. alphabet drill.

7. Which was *not* listed as a word bank activity?

    A. Tracing letters in the words
    B. Word sorts
    C. Alphabetizing
    D. Card games

8. Which one of the following is *not* given for avoiding teaching vocabulary before the children read?

   A. Children can apply word analysis skills.
   B. It saves time.
   C. They cannot learn it any other way.
   D. They might use context skills.

9. Story maps serve what function?

   A. Identify important elements
   B. Show relationships among significant details
   C. Show how texts are structured
   D. All of the above

10. Which is *not* a PReP step?

    A. Brainstorm
    B. Categorize
    C. Rewrite the items
    D. Expand on the attributes in the categories

11. QARs are metacognitive in that they

    A. teach children to verbalize how they know an answer is true.
    B. help the teacher ask better questions.
    C. help the children get the right answers.
    D. all of the above.

12. Which is *not* true about teacher questions?

    A. They should test literal information.
    B. They generally follow the reading of a story.
    C. They should guide students to develop a map of the story.
    D. They should reflect what you are teaching.

13. Oral reading should be used

    A. to insure that all students know the story.
    B. to assess reading development.
    C. to develop self-confidence in poor readers.
    D. all of the above.

14. Which activity would you use to help a student read a Social Studies chapter that is not well organized?

    A. Outlining
    B. Interactive reading guide
    C. Story map
    D. Graphic post-organizer

15. In the DRTA,

    A. the focus is on making correct predictions.
    B. the reader plays an active role in the reading process.
    C. the teacher determines the student's purpose for reading.
    D. all of the above.

73

1. Which is *not* a recommended practice?

   A. Teaching individual letter sounds before teaching whole words
   B. Teaching main ideas before details
   C. Teaching cause and effect
   D. Teaching about graphic organizers before teaching about outlining

2. Which is true about basals?

   A. Provide scope and sequence of skills
   B. Provide better lessons for direct instruction
   C. Provide suggestions for related readings
   D. All of the above

3. Which of the following are important concepts about print for young children?

   A. Print goes from top to bottom.
   B. Print should make sense.
   C. Print stands for speech.
   D. All of the above.

4. Which step is not included in the dictation of a group experience chart?

   A. Teacher reads back the chart as it was dictated.
   B. Boys and girls read the chart chorally.
   C. Children individually read the parts they recognize.
   D. Teacher checks words for the word banks.

5. Which important step in the LEA is out of sequence?

   A. Child dictates a sentences.
   B. Child has the experience.
   C. Teacher writes child's words.
   D. Teacher and child read the sentence.

6. Which was *not* discussed as a possible concern with a group chart?

   A. A child who dominates with too much language for a group chart
   B. Variant dialect or grammar
   C. Contrast with control of the basal
   D. How excited the child gets seeing his/her language

7. Which step is out of sequence?

   A. Perceives words as patterned letters
   B. Matches letters and sounds
   C. Learns prefixes and suffixes
   D. Learns that syllables combine to form words

8. Which is *not* included as a level of comprehension?

   A. Creative
   B. Literal
   C. "Between the lines"
   D. Applicative

9. Which statement is not recommended as part of DRTA?

   A. Read to a stopping place.
   B. Students set purposes.
   C. Teacher checks on the facts of the story.
   D. Children explain where in the story they found something.

10. The content DRTA differs form a story DRTA in what way?

    A. Students make predictions.
    B. Preview headings, pictures, and subheadings in detail.
    C. Set purposes for reading.
    D. Read for information.

11. Which approach aids comprehension?

    A. DRTA
    B. PREP
    C. Outlining
    D. All of the above

12. Which does *not* represent a level in the QAR?

    A. "It says right here that the car went 100 mph."
    B. "It says they drove for half an hour at that speed. I put the two together."
    C. "I know that from traveling with my brother in a car."
    D. "From the facts in the story it just has to be."

13. Which is *not* a purpose for oral reading?

    A. To assess reading development
    B. To be sure the children are paying attention
    C. To check comprehension
    D. To enhance appreciation of a selection

14. During teacher-student reading conferences, teachers

    A. develop reading knowledge.
    B. develop thinking skills.
    C. teach specific skills.
    D. all of the above.

15. Words that are put in a word bank

    A. must be known at sight.
    B. are changed every month.
    C. are selected by the teachers.
    D. all of the above.

9

Responding to Literature Through Reading and Writing

LECTURE DISCUSSION OUTLINE

FOUNDATIONS FOR LITERATURE-BASED READING AND WRITING IN THE CLASSROOM

Categories of Children's Literature

> Alphabet Books
> Picture Books
> Wordless Books
> Traditional Literature
> Poetry
> Historical Fiction
> Contemporary Realism
> Modern Fantasy
> Informational or Nonfiction Books
> Biography
> Children's Special Interests

The Potential for Students' Response to Literature

> Psychosocial Roots of Response to Literature
> Developmental Response to Literature

LITERATURE-BASED READING AND WRITING

Transition to Literature-Based Reading and Writing

The Basic Elements of Narratives

> Plot
> Characterization
> Setting
> Theme

Resolution
Style
Point of View

The Basic Organization for Expository or Informational Texts

Literature-Based Reading and Writing Response Groups and Group Conferences

A Range of Literature-Based Activities

LITERATURE UNITS: CONSTRUCTING AND CONDUCTING

Steps in Constructing Units

Determining the Unit Goals or Objectives
Determining the Unit's Focus
Collecting the Books
Determining the Primary Range of Activities

Procedure for Conducting the Unit

SAMPLE LITERATURE UNITS

Second Grade: *Friendship*
Sixth Grade: *The 21 Balloons*

SUMMARY

Research into elementary students' responses to literature indicates that students should be exposed to a variety of genres and should respond to their reading through discussion and writing activities, because they have the potential to respond to literature in deep and meaningful ways. They need narrative for the same psychological and social reasons as adults: To make sense of and give meaning to their lives. By relating to the main characters in books, children become more attuned to their own thoughts and feelings as well as those of others. Children need to know that the conflicting emotions they experience have been experienced by others. Findings show that most primary children are capable of the higher-level responses of analysis and generalization that formerly were expected only of intermediate students. Although little research has been done to investigate students' responses to expository texts, we do know that summarizing and relating the new information to the known in a journal or through discussion during and/or after reading significantly affects learning and retention. Informational books which stimulate interest in the content areas should play an equal role with fiction in literature-based programs.

A literature-based reading and writing program begins with a transition time, during which teachers walk students through formats and activities that will be a critical part of instruction. With the whole class the teacher explores terminology and introduces types of questions that will be explored in small response groups. In essence, the teacher begins to establish a framework and a mindset for responding to literature. Read-alouds begin with one story, then move to several related stories, and finally to a book chapter. Questions should gradually increase in number and sophistication.

Response groups play an extremely important role in the literature-based curriculum. Through small-group and class conferences, students develop an appreciation of the elements and themes of narratives and poems, and of the worlds of ideas and information in expository trade books. The questions students are asked during teacher-directed response groups, or are given to pursue independently in groups, are the key to developing this appreciation.

A literature unit, focused on a particular theme or topic and addressing specific objectives, usually comprises a "core" selection of books (or sometimes one book) to which all students are exposed (usually in a read-aloud format). These books are read and discussed "intensively." It also includes a number of related books to be read independently and a wide range of activities for students to analyze and apply the knowledge developed and extended through transactions with the core selection(s). The unit uses all the strategies previously taught in the language arts. Discussion includes response groups, as well as individual and group conferences with the teacher. A unit is constructed by first determining its goals/objectives and then its main focus (theme, topic). Books that comprise the central works of the unit are collected, and the primary types of activities in which the students will engage are determined and their sequence planned. *The WEB (Wonderfully Exciting Books)* is an excellent resource to help teachers plan units. The chapter includes two sample units that show how units are implemented. It also includes a wide range of activities that reflects an active and usually critical approach to literature response through reading and writing.

If teachers are to help students become good readers who value literature, they too must be "hooked on books"—especially children's books. They must be well read in and have a general understanding of the various categories of children's books.

SUPPLEMENTARY DISCUSSION TOPICS

1. In small groups, discuss the cinquain poem assigned to the students and then share some of the concepts, feelings, and discoveries with the whole class.

2. One failing of the basal readers was that teachers saw them as the reading program or the content of the reading curriculum. Structure a classroom activity that teaches about a piece of literature. Discuss the subtle but important differences between this activity and using a piece of literature to teach about life.

3. First, have small groups do a semantic map on SETTING. With the whole class, map and discuss their ideas. The discussion can be quite lively and informative.

4. Students are often seriously concerned about how to handle books containing controversial content. Role-play several situations where an irate parent complains to the teacher or the principal about an objectionable book/story used in class or selected for free reading.

5. Bring in *Where the Wild Things Are*. Have the students read it and discuss it as a piece of children's literature. Then tell the class this was a controversial book in the seventies. Ask them to suggest *why* they think it may have been controversial. Discuss censorship of books, stories, and/or ideas.

6. Select a simple piece of children's literature. Develop a study guide for the character's name, a character trait, and lines from the story that show the trait. Have the students read the story and complete the guide. Then conduct a group discussion of their work.

7. Bring a curriculum guide to class and walk through your thinking processes for developing a literature unit. Out of the guide choose some goals/objectives to be addressed. With the class select a topic/theme for a literature unit. Select "core" books and the related books that could be used to reach the objectives/goals. Select and plan the activities of the unit.

STUDENT ACTIVITIES

1. Have the students write a cinquain poem on Chapter 9, as suggested for earlier chapters.

2. Have the students observe a literature lesson in a classroom. In two pages they can describe the materials and activities the teacher used. They should also decide if the teacher was using the literature to teach a particular child or was focusing on literature itself.

3. Have the students select a piece of children's literature. In two pages they can decide which literary parts (character, conflict, theme, setting) they might especially enjoy teaching and share ideas on how they would do so.

4. Have the students examine four or more books on a common theme (friendship). The books should be at different reading levels. Then have them compare how the author uses characterization, setting, and conflict to develop the theme.

5. Have each student write a *lesson plan* for developing one literary skill. If this is done in small groups, then students in each group can base their lesson plans on different skills. The plans can be run off and shared. Students will have the "core" of a literature unit for several books.

6. Have each student select a list of recommended readings (for example, one from Nancy Larrick, Jim Trelease, or the text.). Read two books from at least four categories. In a two-page paper, students should state the list they used, why the books fit into the assigned categories, and then compare the categories to those of the text.

7. Have each student develop a plan for a literature unit, following the four steps presented in this chapter.

1. Which of the following are advantages to teaching literature intensively supplemented with word analysis?

   A. Students tend to read more.
   B. The quality of students' language is more advanced.
   C. Students' attitude toward reading is more positive.
   D. All of the above.

2. Historical fiction is powerful because

   A. historical characters play a main part in the story.
   B. the characters deal with universal problems.
   C. it can deal with any historical era.
   D. the historical parts are accurate.

3. To encounter problems about growing up, a child might read in which category?

   A. Biography
   B. Contemporary realism
   C. Modern fantasy
   D. All of the above

4. Using Erikson's stages of psychosocial development, which is the most likely choice for a nine-year-old?

   A. A book about friendship and trust
   B. A book about feeling guilty
   C. A book about hard work paying off
   D. None of the above

5. Which is *not* a critical factor about the "read-alouds"?

   A. Introduce terminology.
   B. Develop questioning strategies.
   C. Establish a mindset for analyzing literature.
   D. Teach one of the specific reading skills.

6. Which does *not* fit with ideas given in the text for showing overall reaction to a book?

   A. Write a one-page book report.
   B. Sort a group of books according to categories.
   C. Rate a book on an excitement scale.
   D. Write the dialogue for a picture book.

7. Which is *not* a basic element of narrative?

   A. Characterization
   B. Details
   C. Setting
   D. Resolution

8. Which of the following is not appropriate for developing thinking skills?

   A. Compare parts of a current book to the same parts of (a) previous book(s).
   B. Structure interpretive questions for which there are no direct answers.
   C. Fill in a worksheet on cause and effect.
   D. Students conduct DLTAs and DRTAs from selections.

9. Which is *not* an element of a literature unit?

   A. It uses many pages from the skills program.
   B. It involves all the strategies for reading and writing.
   C. It lasts for an extended period of time.
   D. It involves all the language arts.

10. Which is *not* a feature of setting?

    A. Time
    B. Plot
    C. Place
    D. Mood

11. Which is *not* an appropriate response-group activity?

    A. Prepare responses to a study guide.
    B. Deal with a dilemma about the conflict.
    C. Write a play.
    D. Consider complicating factors.

12. Which reflects a literature-centered curriculum?

    A. "Students who read more are better readers."
    B. "Students who read real literature are more positive toward reading."
    C. "Students in a literature-centered program tend to read more."
    D. All of the above.

13. Which of the following best describes contemporary literature?

    A. It avoids controversy.
    B. It addresses current concerns in an historical context.
    C. It can address just about any problem or concern.
    D. It is primarily expository.

14. Which type of story is chosen most frequently by intermediate students?

    A. Mysteries
    B. Family situations
    C. Animal stories
    D. Folk tales

15. Informational books

    A. play a minor role in literature-based units.
    B. are most appropriate for at-home reading.
    C. get many children "hooked on books."
    D. all of the above.

1. Which type of book may be *out of place* in a preschool classroom?

    A. Alphabet books
    B. Historical fiction
    C. Picture books
    D. Big Books

2. To get more background on space travel, a child might read in which category?

    A. Biography
    B. Informational
    C. Science fiction
    D. All of the above

3. Which factor seems most important for developing higher levels of responses to literature?

    A. Retelling the story
    B. Writing about the story
    C. Using content material
    D. None of the above

4. In place of teaching a piece of literature, the teacher might use it for what purpose(s)?

    A. Sample a genre
    B. Follow a theme
    C. Compare it to another work
    D. All of the above

5. Which is the simplest task in a literature program?

    A. Decide if statements can be justified from the text.
    B. Solve a social dilemma.
    C. Sequence the events of a story.
    D. Compare story details with something current.

6. Which is effective in following up on characterization?

    A. Take the perspective from the villain's view.
    B. Make a list of the characters in a story and name one trait.
    C. Write in a response journal as the character from a book.
    D. Introduce characters from a book to the class.

7. Which step is out of sequence in constructing a literature unit?

    A. Gather the materials.
    B. Determine the goals.
    C. Determine the main focus of the unit.
    D. Determine the range of activities.

8. Which is *not* a type of conflict in a story?

   A. A heavy rain, causing a flood
   B. Between one character and another
   C. Man against nature
   D. Man struggling against his own limitations

9. Which is *not* a pattern for informational texts?

   A. East to west
   B. Start to end
   C. Known to unknown
   D. Easy to difficult

10. Which is *not* usually a topic for modern fantasy?

    A. Existence of God
    B. Growing up
    C. Folk tales
    D. None of the above

11. In general, primary students choose

    A. science fiction.
    B. biographies.
    C. animal stories.
    D. poetry.

12. Which would be most influential in making a literature-based reading program successful?

    A. A large school library
    B. A requirement of four book reports per month
    C. A teacher who values literature
    D. A skills tracking system

13. During transition to a primarily literature-based curriculum

    A. levels of questions are unimportant.
    B. read-alouds begin with easy chapter books.
    C. students are prepared for small-group work.
    D. all of the above.

14. Using Erikson's stages of psychosocial development, which would a five-year-old most likely want to listen to?

    A. A book about friendship and trust
    B. A book where someone feels guilty
    C. A book where hard work pays off
    D. None of the above

15. Literature-based response groups

    A. focus on higher-level questions.
    B. deal only with the elements of narratives.
    C. are not teacher-directed.
    D. all of the above.

10

The Teaching of Vocabulary and Spelling

LECTURE DISCUSSION OUTLINE

PRINCIPLES FOR LEARNING AND TEACHING VOCABULARY

VOCABULARY DEVELOPMENT IN THE PRIMARY GRADES

Elaborating and Expanding Conceptual Development

    Developing Vocabulary and Concepts Through Word Sorts

VOCABULARY DEVELOPMENT IN THE INTERMEDIATE GRADES

Learning How the Structure of Words Represents Meaning

    Morphemic Elements
        Prefixes, Suffixes, and Base Words
        Stems: Word Roots and Combining Forms
    Etymology
        Indo-European Roots of Words
        Words form Greek and Roman Mythology
        Changing Word Meanings
        Role of the Dictionary in Etymology

Presenting and Reinforcing Content-related Vocabulary

    Dictionary Use

Working with Categories of Language Use

    Synonyms
    Denotation and Connotation
    Similes and Metaphors
    Homonyms
    Antonyms
    Analogies

THE FOUNDATIONS OF LEARNING AND TEACHING SPELLING

Three Principles of English Spelling

Developmental Acquisition of Spelling Knowledge

> Semiphonemic and Letter Name Stages
> Within-Word Pattern Stage
> Syllable Juncture Stage
> Derivational Patterns Stage

Formal Spelling Instruction

> Letter Name
> Within-Word Pattern
> Syllable Juncture
> Derivational Patterns: The Spelling-Meaning Connection

Organization of Formal Instruction

Informal Spelling Instruction

SUMMARY

The teaching of vocabulary and spelling are addressed in the same chapter because the two are intertwined. Vocabulary knowledge helps spelling development, while spelling knowledge helps expand vocabulary. During the last twenty-five years research has changed our thinking about the efficiency of our spelling system and how children learn to spell. Because spelling plays such an important role in the language arts, teachers need to understand how the system is structured and children's developmental spelling process, in order for instruction to benefit students.

The most effective way to develop vocabulary is to read extensively . Reading presents words in a natural context, provides repeated exposures necessary for deeper processing, provides more exposure to new terms and concepts than possible in any type of vocabulary "program," and provides exposure to variant forms of base words so the extensions of meaning are illustrated and reinforced. Informal wordplay and word exploration through direct teaching also contribute to vocabulary growth. Vocabulary development has two facets: elaboration—the growth of existing concepts associated with particular words—and expansion—the development of new concepts/vocabulary. There are seven fundamental principles for teaching vocabulary: 1) integrate word study with prior knowledge and learning in content areas; 2) study "some" words intensively with repeated exposure in meaningful context; 3) teach through direct instruction and "teacher talk"; 4) actively involve students in instruction; 5) teach strategies for independent learning; 6) teach words in "families"; and 7) appropriately sequence the teaching of word elements.

Vocabulary development in the primary grades grows out of the oral language that surrounds children, the written language of the read-alouds, and the concrete examination of the here-and-now world of primary students. Instruction should begin by thoroughly examining and elaborating existing, familiar concepts, and then proceed to new information/concepts/vocabulary. Concrete "hands on," experiences, pictures, films, and modeling of vocabulary by the teacher are ways to teach new vocabulary. Teachers should also talk about words in and of themselves, showing students that words can be enjoyed and are interesting. Word sorts are particularly effective for specific exploration of sight vocabulary, corresponding concepts, and knowledge about word structure. They may be "open" or "closed" and done in a group or individually.

The most direct and systematic vocabulary development begins during the intermediate grades. Instruction now focuses on developing knowledge in morphemic or structural analysis following this sequence of instruction: compound words, then prefixes and suffixes, and finally word stems. The study of word origins also contributes to vocabulary development, with Greek and Roman mythology providing exciting content. The study of how and why the meanings of words change is yet another area for vocabulary development. Finally, the study of synonyms, antonyms, the distinction between denotation and connotation, analogies, and figurative language help students to understand written language more clearly because they are able to make finer distinctions about meaning. Structured overviews, semantic maps, and semantic feature analysis are effective ways to preteach content-related vocabulary that cannot be independently learned through context. Words that have been selected for direct instruction need to be reinforced in productive ways such as word association and sentence completion.

Our spelling system is governed by three general principles: 1) the *alphabetic principle*, which states that letters represent sounds in a more or less left-to-right correspondence; 2) the *within-word pattern principle*, which states that the sounds that particular letters or groups of letters represent depend on either the effects of other letters in the word or the position of the sounds; and 3) the *meaning principle*, which states that meaning elements within words are usually spelled consistently. Contrary to the previously accepted idea that spelling is a word-specific, rote-memory process, research has shown that learning to spell is a developmental process with distinct stages. As children attempt to write, they subconsciously construct the rules that govern our spelling system. These stages can be identified by analyzing children's invented spellings. Children begin at the semiphonemic stage, which is characterized by the use of recognizable letters and the representation of some sounds in words (usually only consonants). In the second stage, the letter-name stage, children represent most of the sounds in a word, but they use the articulatory features of the names of the letters to select the graphic representations. They operate in terms of the alphabetic principle. In the third stage, the within-word pattern stage, children master short vowel spellings and move to examining the way long vowels are represented. They will understand most of the basic within-word single-syllable patterns before they move on. The fourth stage is the syllable juncture stage, where children begin to master the conventions that govern the joining of syllables, prefixes, and suffixes in high-frequency words. In the last stage, the derivational patterns stage, the student understands and is able to apply the fundamental meaning principle that words related in meaning are often spelled similarly even though they *sound* different. The chapter includes specific teaching strategies for each developmental level. For formal spelling, lists of words are grouped or categorized according to a common pattern or principle. The pretest/self-correct/study/posttest format with spaced review is recommended for optimal learning.

SUPPLEMENTARY DISCUSSION TOPICS

1. Select a passage on vocabulary and construct a cloze task by deleting every fifth word, after the first sentence is complete. With the class, work through the first paragraph, showing them how to do a cloze task. Let them complete the rest of the

task in small groups. Then you can lead a discussion on the process of doing a cloze task or on the content of the passage. Ultimately, you might want to show how cloze can be a great vocabulary-building exercise.

2. For so many years spelling has been phonic-based and memorization-oriented. It may sound as if whole language advocates are saying, "Throw out all drills in skills. Show how a traditional spelling approach does not fit the philosophy of integrated language instruction. Then show how a sensible spelling program does.

3. Create a crossword puzzle on the vocabulary terms of this chapter or from the entire book. As a class project show your students how to use the various clues as strategies for solving the puzzle. Then discuss how the same technique can be effective in the elementary grades.

4. Present samples of children's writing with various "invented" spellings. Discuss the concept of "invented" spelling. Analyze the nonstandard spellings to show how they reflect the developmental stage of the writer.

5. Discuss with the class how they will merge the concepts of invented spelling in the primary grades and *formal* spelling instruction, as has been generally taught in the past.

6. Discuss the issue of intensive word study with a limited number of words versus memorizing an extensive number of words.

7. Discuss the preteaching of vocabulary in literature or other content materials. You might do a think-aloud to show your students how you determine which words need instruction and which do not.

STUDENT ACTIVITIES

1. Have the students create crossword puzzles on the vocabulary of this chapter. *Crossword Magic* is a reasonable commercial program that is easy to use. They might distribute their puzzles and work several.

2. Have your students observe in the classroom for vocabulary-building lessons or exercises. They can write a two-page paper about what they observe, including the attitude of the students toward the activity.

3. Have your students observe some spelling lessons in the classroom. They should write a two-page paper describing the list of words, the types of activities the children did, and the attitude of the students toward the activities.

4. Have your students observe some writing activities in classrooms. Have them write a two-page paper describing: 1) how the children deal with spelling "problems" during the writing, and 2) how the teacher helps. Then comment on the effectiveness of the spelling program in getting the children to accurately encode spelling words in their writing activities.

5. Have your students analyze a current spelling series (from their local schools or from a curriculum library). In a two-page paper, have them comment on the ideas in the series and compare the program to the ideas expressed in this chapter.

6. Have your students look at the dictionaries used in a classroom and see if they are of the newer type described in this chapter. Then they can find five words that have an interesting etymology, create structured overviews or maps of them, and share them with peers.

7. Have your students select one of the references for using mythology in vocabulary building. They can pick a word that has its root in mythology. In a paper they should summarize the information about that word, map out what is important, and share it with peers, in order to build a resource file on this kind of activity.

89

1. Having a child merely copy the definition of an "unknown" word from a dictionary violates which fundamental principle of vocabulary development?

    A. Teachers should engage in a good deal of explicit teacher talk.
    B. Word study should be integrated with prior knowledge.
    C. Word study should involve intensive, deep study of some words.
    D. All of the above.

2. Considering the principle of moving form the known to the unknown, with which map drawing experience should a teacher begin?

    A. The classroom
    B. The student's house
    C. The neighborhood
    D. The town

3. Which would *not* be a part of word sorting for vocabulary development?

    A. Alphabetizing
    B. Categorizing
    C. Elaborating
    D. Using known words

4. Which is *not* discussed for expanding vocabulary in content areas?

    A. Glossary work
    B. Structured overview
    C. Semantic maps
    D. Sentence completion

5. Which is *not* a feature of the semantic map discussion?

    A. Brainstorming
    B. Categorizing the terms
    C. Teacher adding terms
    D. Using the dictionary

6. Which is out of sequence in the semantic feature analysis?

    A. Put feature words across top and target words down the side.
    B. Discuss and develop the matrix.
    C. Point out how reading the matrix is beneficial.
    D. Build the bridges between the known and unknown.

7. Which is *not* characteristic of dictionaries?

    A. They supply information about meanings of words.
    B. They are the best tools for expanding students' vocabularies.
    C. They give etymological information (beyond primary grades).
    D. They provide major pronunciation keys.

8. Which is *not* discussed as a vocabulary-building activity?

   A. Analyzing and developing similes and metaphors
   B. Looking up lists of spelling words in the dictionary
   C. Working with analogies
   D. Developing synonyms

9. Which is *not* a feature of a well-constructed spelling series?

   A. It teaches the rules of god phonic generalizations.
   B. The scope and sequence correlate with the word study program.
   C. It goes beyond mere rote memorization.
   D. It provides appropriate word lists.

10. The different sounds represented by the "gh" in the words "ghost" and "tough" are explained by which principle of English spelling?

    A. Alphabetic
    B. Within-word
    C. Meaning
    D. None of the above

11. Which steps are what Henderson calls the spelling cycle for teaching memorization of words?

    A. Pretest followed by self-correction
    B. Study followed by posttest
    C. Spaced review
    D. All of the above

12. Which activity does *not* belong with the syllable juncture stage?

    A. The examination of stressed syllables
    B. The examination of more complex prefixes and suffixes
    C. The examination of different vowel alternations
    D. The examination of stressed syllables

13. The use of the word "Xerox" for "photocopy" represents word change by

    A. degeneration.
    B. elevation.
    C. generalization.
    D. specialization.

14. The sentence "A big tre fal on mi bik" ("A big tree fell on my bike") represents which stage of spelling?

    A. Semiphonemic
    B. Letter-name
    C. Within-word pattern
    D. Syllable juncture

15. In vocabulary acquisition, which is the most difficult?

    A. Inflectional endings
    B. Simple prefixes
    C. Compound words
    D. Affixes attached to word stems

1. Having a child merely copy the definition of an "unknown" word from a dictionary violates which fundamental principle of vocabulary development?

    A. It should involve many exposures in meaningful contexts.
    B. Words should be taught in meaningful "families."
    C. Word study should be integrated with learning in content areas.
    D. All of the above.

2. Which is *not* a sound step in expanding conceptual frameworks?

    A. Pair labels and language with concrete experiences.
    B. Say the word and have the children repeat it.
    C. Model the language.
    D. Talk about words.

3. Which vocabulary-building activity is the most difficult?

    A. Expanding conceptual development
    B. Meaning from compound words
    C. Meaning from attaching affixes to base words
    D. Meaning by attaching affixes to stems

4. Which is *not* appropriate for instruction in the primary grades?

    A. Compound words
    B. Simple prefixes
    C. Simple suffixes
    D. Word stems

5. Which is *not* one of the forms of word change?

    A. Centralization
    B. Generalization
    C. Elevation
    D. Degeneration

6. Which is *not* as effective a means of expanding vocabulary in content areas?

    A. Semantic feature analysis
    B. Sentence completion
    C. Dictionary
    D. Semantic map

7. Which is *not* a part of the semantic map?

    A. It develops from categorizing.
    B. It sequences concepts.
    C. It activates prior knowledge.
    D. It displays children's knowledge.

8. Which is *not* discussed as a vocabulary-building activity?

    A. Exploring metaphors
    B. Differentiating denotation from connotation
    C. Looking up lists of spelling words in the dictionary
    D. Working with antonyms, synonyms, and homonyms

9. Which is *not* a feature of a well-constructed spelling series?

    A. It focuses on teaching the most frequent, irregularly-spelled words.
    B. It examines words from a variety of perspectives.
    C. It leads to spelling generalizations.
    D. It reinforces the spelling/meaning connection.

10. "Steak" and "stake" are explained by which principle of English spelling?

    A. Alphabetic
    B. Within-word
    C. Meaning
    D. None of the above

11. Which activity does *not* belong with the letter-name stage?

    A. Substitution of beginning consonants
    B. Comparing two spellings of long *e*
    C. Grouping by beginning digraph
    D. Focus on recognition of letters

12. Which is *not* a part of the weekly spelling cycle?

    A. Teacher corrects tests
    B. Study of words
    C. Scheduled reviews
    D. Pretest

13. The sentence "I liek to eet choklit ice creem" ("I like to eat chocolate ice cream") represents which stage of spelling?

    A. Letter-name
    B. Within-word pattern
    C. Syllable juncture
    D. Derivational patterns

14. Which statement is *not* true regarding semantic feature analysis?

    A. It primarily deals with lower-level thinking skills.
    B. It allows for examination of concepts in relation to one another.
    C. It is a categorizing activity.
    D. It may be used with small groups or the whole class.

15. Which step is out of sequence in the spelling-meaning walk-through?

    A. Write "inspire and inspiration" on the board.
    B. Have students compare auditory and visual presentations.
    C. Choose other, similar examples.
    D. Talk about the meaning of the two words.

11

The Teaching of Grammar and Handwriting

GRAMMAR

A Tale of Four Grammars

> Traditional Grammar
> Structural Grammar
> Transformational-Generative Grammar
> Case Grammar

Teaching Grammar

> Parts of Speech
> Sentences
>> Sentence Expansion
>> Sentence Combining

USAGE

Standard English and Dialects

> Role Playing
> Adapted Language Experience Approach
> Read-alouds
> Discussion

MECHANICS

HANDWRITING

Handwriting in Preschool and Kindergarten

Handwriting Styles

Teaching Manuscript and Cursive Writing

Evaluating Handwriting

Maintaining Interest in Handwriting

SUMMARY

Grammar and usage are learned to help us understand and appreciate the potential of the language, not as conventions to be studied in their own right. They enable writers to express thoughts more creatively and effectively. When instruction in grammar and usage occurs as part of the revising and editing phases or as part of a real social context, learning is relevant and appropriate. Historically there have been three schools of grammar—traditional, structural, and transformational-generative. Traditional grammar dates to when scholars tried to make English as much like Latin as possible. Our labels for parts of speech and many rules for usage originated during this period. Traditional study includes labeling parts of speech, identifying and labeling types of clauses, and diagramming sentences. Structural grammar emerged during the first half of the twentieth century and focused on how people used language. Structural grammarians identified four form classes of words, based on the functions these words filled in sentences, and some basic sentence patterns. Transformational-generative grammar is a theory that tries to identify a finite set of rules by which people are able to generate an infinite number of sentences. There are basic sentence patterns, termed kernel sentences, which are transformed to express thought. The kernel sentences are constructed by some simple rules in the "deep structure" of language and are transformed by another set of rules to "surface structure" characterized by speech or writing. The primary effect of transformational-generative grammar on instruction has been in the areas of sentence expansion and sentence combining.

Instruction must proceed from the concrete to the abstract. The general sequence for teaching parts of speech is as follows: 1) proper nouns; 2) common nouns; 3) verbs; 4) adjectives; 5) pronouns; 6) articles or determiners; 7) adverbs; 8) prepositions; and 9) conjunctions. Labeling the parts of speech enables the teacher and students to talk about the words writers use. "Silly Syntax," generation of compound words, word sorts, "Grammatical Terms: What's in a Name?," and poetry are activities that help develop awareness of and knowledge about parts of speech.

The developmental sequence for the examination of sentences is as follows: 1) understanding the concept of a sentence; 2) attending to the order of words; 3) understanding basic subject/predicate division; 4) recognizing specific subjects and predicates in simple sentences and then expanding those "kernel" sentences; 5) contracting and combining longer sentences; and 6) linking sentences together with logical connectives. The value of developing students' understanding of sentences by identifying and manipulating phrases lies not only in making their responses to the different structures in writing more automatic, but also in the critical thinking and deeper-level reasoning that occur as part of that process. The two most important strategies for developing thought and expression are sentence expansion and sentence combining. Sentence building is a particularly effective activity for expanding sentences. Sentence combination can be addressed by "walking through" the process of sentence combining with students using short, "kernel"-type sentences that have graphic and word "cues" for combining. Both the reading the students do and the read-alouds by the teacher provide the best models of different types of sentence constructions.

The metalanguage of grammar makes discussion of usage easier. Some elements of usage should be known automatically. These should be presented through direct teaching and reinforced in the revision and editing stages. Others are not important enough to address directly. In those instances, consulting a usage guide is the best strategy. Basal language arts/English series can be effective sources for guides on usage. The most important aspect of usage is the issue of standard English and variant English dialects. Teachers must be understanding of the variant dialects, but at the same time help students learn standard English. In addition to the teacher as a model, role playing, adapted language experience approach, read-alouds, and discussion help students learn standard English.

The purpose for handwriting instruction is to ensure that students learn to write legibly and automatically. Less time needs to be spent on direct instruction, more time on allowing students opportunities to apply what they are learning about handwriting. The guiding principles for handwriting instruction are: 1) be consistent; 2) be a good model; 3) clearly display the model of the style being used in the classroom; and 4) emphasize "real" writing. Before writing instruction is begun, students' "play writing" must be clearly developed; they should have established hand dominance; they should be able to use crayons, scissors, and pencils; and they should be able to copy shapes. Initial instruction should include the correct way to hold a pencil and to position the paper. Modeling and guided observation are the best methods for instruction. The sequence for introducing letters should be organized according to shared features. Evaluation of handwriting should focus on: 1) letter formation; 2) size and proportion; 3) spacing; 4) slant; 5) alignment; and 6) line quality. To create interest in handwriting, introduce students to calligraphy, graphology, and other historical "writing" methods.

SUPPLEMENTARY DISCUSSION TOPICS

1. Construct a cloze task from a passage in the chapter. Work on the syntactic cues for selecting the words for the blanks. If you have not done this before, look at the suggestions for the first one in the "Supplementary Discussion Topics" in Chapter 10.

2. Develop a semantic map on GRAMMAR. The ensuing discussion could be quite enlightening for you and your students.

3. Discuss with the class issues in dealing with variant dialects, especially how to tactfully "correct" someone. Then role-play a situation where a student uses nonstandard constructions and a teacher sensitively encourages the child to use the standard ones.

4. Create a crossword puzzle on the vocabulary terms of this chapter. As a class project show your students how to use the various clues as strategies for solving the puzzle. Then discuss how the same technique can be effective in the elementary grades.

5. Play tapes or show transcripts of children's oral language and share writing samples. Then show how a teacher might use the traditional grammar book in prescriptive ways to deal with the children's language needs.

6. If a teacher does not watch young children forming and practicing letter writing, it is likely that some children will practice them in awkward ways. You might talk about how handwriting practice can help children with dominance problems and directionality.

7. Do some of the grammar activities mentioned in the chapter and show how a grammar lesson can be fun and instructive at the same time. Discuss the strengths and weaknesses of the activities with the students.

STUDENT ACTIVITIES

1. Have your students develop manuscript and cursive skills by selecting an appropriate system and practicing it until you certify they can serve as a model for the children. You might ask for a paper in which the students compare their letter formation to what is expected in the writing system they chose. You want to have them decide if their own style is acceptable against the standard they will teach.

2. Have your students observe in the classroom for grammar lessons or exercises. They can write a two-page paper about what they observe, including the attitude of the students toward the activity.

3. Have the students search printed materials and interview teachers to develop a teacher file on activities to develop small motor skills as writing readiness.

4. Have your students observe in the classroom for writing lessons. In a two-page paper, they should describe how the teacher differentiates activities and instruction to accommodate the wide spread of skills in grammar and writing.

5. Have the students create crossword puzzles on the vocabulary of this chapter. *Crossword Magic* is a reasonable commercial program that is easy to use. They might distribute their puzzles and work several.

6. Have the students pick from the suggestions or games for teaching grammar. They can develop an activity or lesson to teach to peers in small groups. By this time the peers might be expected to give helpful feedback, if you have used a lot of small-group interactions in your class.

95

1. Which is *not* one of the three approaches to grammar?

   A. Colonial
   B. Traditional
   C. Transformational-generative
   D. Structural

2. Which term is *not* associated with the traditional grammar system?

   A. Nouns
   B. Determiners
   C. Prescriptive
   D. Diagramming

3. Which term is *not* associated with the transformational-generative grammar system?

   A. Kernel sentence
   B. Chomsky
   C. Surface structure
   D. Prescriptive

4. In teaching about grammar, which is the least abstract concept?

   A. Adverbs
   B. Adjectives
   C. Nouns
   D. Verbs

5. Which is an appropriate activity for teaching about prepositions?

   A. Word sorting
   B. Direct teaching lesson
   C. "Silly Syntax"
   D. All of the above

6. Which is *not* an appropriate sentence expansion activity?

   A. Movability exercises from an English book
   B. Sentence diagramming
   C. Peer group feedback on writing
   D. Sentence building from literature

7. Which activity seems the simplest way for combining two ideas?

   A. Join them by "and."
   B. Collapse one idea to an adjective and combine it with the other.
   C. Relate an idea to another with a relative pronoun.
   D. Subordinate one idea to another.

8. What makes a dialect standard?

   A. It is the language of the majority of our society.
   B. It is the language of the rich in our society.
   C. It is the language of those who have succeeded in our society.
   D. It is the appropriate language for our society.

9. Which is an appropriate activity for teaching standard English?

   A. Diagramming sentences
   B. Language experience approach
   C. Role playing
   D. All of the above

10. Which is *not* emphasized for handwriting?

    A. Be a good model.
    B. Provide plenty of practice.
    C. Be consistent.
    D. Emphasize real writing.

11. Manuscript is preferred over cursive for beginners because

    A. it looks like printed letters.
    B. it is easier for young children.
    C. the bonding features of manuscript are helpful.
    D. all of the above.

12. Which is *not* a sign that a child is ready for writing instruction?

    A. The child can write and spell his/her name correctly.
    B. Hand dominance is established.
    C. Small-muscle dexterity is accomplished.
    D. "Play writing" is clear.

13. Which features are judged in handwriting?

    A. Spacing
    B. Slant
    C. Size and proportion
    D. All of the above

14. Precise labels for parts of speech

    A. enable students to discuss writing more easily.
    B. do not need to be learned if the concepts are understood.
    C. should be used when first introducing the concepts.
    D. all of the above.

15. Diagramming sentences

    A. is a very effective method for teaching parts of sentences.
    B. develops positive attitudes about writing.
    C. can be fun for students interested in analyzing language.
    D. all of the above.

1. Which term is *not* associated with the structural grammar system?

   A. Determiners
   B. Bloomfield
   C. Pronouns
   D. Descriptive

2. Which term is *not* associated with the case grammar system?

   A. Chomsky
   B. Meaning is central
   C. Verb is core
   D. Agentive

3. In the sequence from most concrete to most abstract, which is out of order?

   A. Nouns
   B. Prepositions
   C. Verbs
   D. Adjectives

4. Which is an appropriate activity for teaching about adjectives?

   A. "Silly Syntax"
   B. Word sorts
   C. Sentence frames
   D. All of the above

5. The _____ sentence is the middle stage of sentence writing.

   A. complete
   B. kernel
   C. expanded
   D. complicated

6. Which is the preferred term for a dialect different from the standard?

   A. Nonstandard
   B. Variant
   C. Inferior
   D. Inappropriate

7. What do children know about writing, before formal instruction begins?

   A. Directionality of print
   B. Recurrence of characters
   C. Generativity
   D. All of the above

8. Which step is *not* a part of the suggested sequence for directly teaching handwriting?

   A. Model and guide observation
   B. Apply and verbalize
   C. Evaluate the results
   D. Compare with model

9. Which is *not* a part of how to hold a pencil for writing?

   A. The child should be comfortable holding the pencil.
   B. Left-handed students should rotate the wrist.
   C. The hand does not cover the line of print during the writing.
   D. Forefinger, middle finger, and thumb are in contact with the pencil.

10. The underlying premise for teaching grammar and usage is that they

    A. enable students to express thoughts more clearly.
    B. make students better spellers.
    C. are a required school subject.
    D. enable students to diagram sentences.

11. According to the text, the study of grammar has not been popular with students because

    A. grammar exercises were used for disciplinary purposes.
    B. too much time was spent on its instruction.
    C. the textbooks were too difficult.
    D. they were not taught how to apply their grammatical knowledge.

12. "Silly Syntax" and word sorts are effective activities to reinforce knowledge of parts of speech because they

    A. rely on the use of a textbook.
    B. take very little time.
    C. do not seem to be instructional.
    D. do not require teacher involvement.

13. When teaching standard English to intermediate students who speak variant dialects,

    A. identify and correct all nonstandard constructions.
    B. select constructions for correction from students' writing.
    C. target instruction for the drafting or composing stage.
    D. all of the above.

14. Current handwriting instruction is different from instruction in the past, in that today

    A. more time is spent on instruction.
    B. less time is spent on instruction.
    C. more emphasis is placed on exact replication of the model.
    D. less time is spent on application.

15. Students should understand that the purpose of working with sentence combining is to

    A. diagram sentences.
    B. write more effective expository papers.
    C. better understand the parts of speech.
    D. better express ideas.

12

Assessment and Evaluation of Students' Instructional Needs

LECTURE DISCUSSION OUTLINE

PERSPECTIVES AND DEFINITIONS

INFORMAL ASSESSMENT AND EVALUATION

Oral Language

Writing

    Portfolio Assessment in Writing
        First Grade
        Second Grade
        Third Grade
        Fourth, Fifth, and Sixth Grades

Reading

    Grouping and Making Initial Decisions
    Informal Reading Inventories (IRIs)
    Portfolio Assessment in Reading
        Attitudes and Understanding about Reading
        Responses to Literature Tasks
        Running Record

Spelling

    Forming Initial Judgments of Students' Knowledge
    Ongoing Assessment and Evaluation

FORMAL ASSESSMENT AND EVALUATION

Reading

    Traditional Standardized Group Tests

The "New Generation" of Standardized Group Tests

Writing

Standardized Group Tests

SUMMARY

Assessment and evaluation play significant roles in the educational world. Informal assessment and evaluation are classroom-based and of more value to teachers, because they are the best means for determining both student growth and instructional direction. They are used to determine students' strengths and weaknesses, to form groups, and to determine what students have learned in order to plan for future instruction. Formal assessment and evaluation involve the administration and interpretation of standardized tests to determine how well large groups of students are doing in specific subject areas. This information is used by local school boards and at the state and national levels for a variety of purposes.

Throughout the year teachers informally assess and evaluate students' oral and written language growth through teacher-made tests, informal inventories, and observational notes made when interacting with students individually or in groups. Portfolio assessment is an effective and popular way for teachers to evaluate students and for students to evaluate themselves in the language arts. Portfolios include samples of work selected by the student and teacher, observational notes by the teacher, the student's own assessments, and progress notes contributed by teacher and student.

Oral language is assessed through group and one-to-one interactions, including the spoken language of students working without teacher involvement. Teachers should evaluate how well students are able to express themselves through appropriate use of syntax and vocabulary and to rephrase when their meaning is unclear. They should also observe how well students comprehend others, and if they articulate correctly, participate in group discussions, and play with using language structures and vocabulary that come from their reading or read-alouds. Observation notes should be included in the assessment portfolio.

A student's development in the writing process is assessed through observing the student working with groups, a partner, or individually, and through teacher/student conferences. This information should be included in the student's writing folder, periodically reviewed with the student, and transferred to the assessment portfolio. Only selected compositions should be graded, and much of the evaluation should be holistic. The chapter includes specific guidelines for evaluating writing in grades one through six. Some student-selected compositions should be included in the assessment portfolio, and, if desired, a skills checklist for tracking student progress.

Although most of the time students work in heterogeneous groups, for some direct teaching in reading, students are grouped homogeneously by reading proficiency. Initially, these groups are formed by informally observing students' choices of books during SSR, "spot checking" how well they are handling the books by having them read a paragraph aloud, and doing DRTAs with students who seem to be of similar ability. More specific and detailed information about students' reading can be obtained through an Informal Reading Inventory (IRI). IRIs may be used early in the school year with students who are significantly behind their peers. Throughout the year they may be used with all students to evaluate strengths and weaknesses. Information about students' attitudes and understandings about reading and their responses to literature tasks that assess growth in comprehension should be included in the assessment portfolio. This information can come from the Voluntary Reading Log, a list of skills and strategies that have been taught, and comments based on observations during individual and group conferences. Information about students' development of word analysis ability in context, as well as reading fluency and expression, can also be included in the portfolio through the use of a "running record."

Just as with reading, an initial assessment of spelling knowledge should be done in order to group students for instruction. This assessment should provide information about students' word knowledge and appropriate placement for word study. The assessment may be in the form of a placement test that is included in the basal spelling series or an informal spelling inventory. Throughout the year, students' developmental spelling or word knowledge can be assessed through the weekly spelling tests and through informal observation of students' writing. The writing samples in the assessment portfolios, especially the spontaneous writing, also provide ongoing information.

Significant efforts are underway to change the nature of formal assessment and evaluation as well as the public's perception of educational testing. One possible way to begin this change would be to collect more information from fewer students in order to include authentic writing and reading tasks across a range of different purposes—now only considered informal assessments. Many reading and language arts educators in several states and at the national level are constructing standardized group tests in reading that represent the recent conceptions of the reading process; the reader, the text, and the context must all be considered. The new National Assessment of Education Progress scheduled for 1990 and the Illinois Goal Assessment Program for Reading are examples of the "new generation" of standardized group tests. Formal assessment of writing in recent years has been more realistic than formal reading assessment, primarily because the technique used, holistic evaluation, can be applied to classroom assessment. Not only can holistic scoring be adapted to yield information about the overall coherence, content, and mechanics of a composition, but also about the features specific to different types of writing.

SUPPLEMENTARY DISCUSSION TOPICS

1. With the class, develop a semantic map on TESTING. Attributes in some of the categories can be developed and discussed in small groups, before sharing with the class as a whole. Students generally respond favorably to this activity, especially on testing.

2. As a class project build a crossword puzzle on the terms from this chapter. The students' definitions and cues should be enlightening.

3. Bring in the parent and school reports for a particular student based on a group standardized test. Explain the basic concepts and terms that *might* confuse your students and that are generally misunderstood by parents. Look especially at the grade equivalent score.

4. Role-play how a teacher shares both informal information in the portfolio and standardized test results with parents. Pay particular attention to what happens when children score at the extremes on the standardized tests.

5. Not all societies fit the bell-shaped curve. Not all educational systems accept the assumptions of the bell-shaped distribution. Discuss with the class some of the ramifications the bell-shaped distribution has for other than middle class, Anglo-American students and classrooms.

6. Your students and many parents of elementary children may disagree with portfolio scoring as presented in this chapter. Role-play various situations where the teacher has to explain this kind of system to parents of different acceptance levels. (What will s/he do about not grading every paper or having the students select which ones to grade?)

STUDENT ACTIVITIES

1. Have the students read three explanations of grade-equivalent and of standardized tests. These can include test publishers' technical manuals, journal articles, or chapters in books. On 5" × 7" cards students can summarize the articles and comment on their usefulness.

2. Have students observe in a classroom to determine how the teacher informally assesses and evaluates students. In a two-page paper they should describe the assessment situations, what the teacher and students were doing, and how they reacted to what was going on.

3. Students may interview a teacher regarding his or her use of standardized test information in the language arts. Seek opinions on the usefulness of informal and formal testing. Let the students meet in small groups, share, and then compare their information.

4. Explore examples of and literature on IRIs and Miscue Analysis. Provide tapes or transcripts of children's oral reading, and have your students practice listening for and recording some simple miscues, such as omissions and insertions. Let them explore as deeply as they can in either form of inventory.

5. From five to ten compositions provided by the professor, try to determine one or two skills that a teacher might want to teach directly in literature (such as characterization or setting), or spelling and grammar (including sentence combining and expanding). This might be done in small groups and reported to the whole class.

107

1. Assessment differs from evaluation in that it refers to

    A. selection of tests versus synthesis of information.
    B. administration of tests versus decisions about results.
    C. selection and administration versus synthesis and decisions.
    D. all of the above.

2. Which is *not* an informal assessment and evaluation purpose?

    A. Plan the next instructional task.
    B. Compare one school to other district schools.
    C. Assign grades.
    D. Determine students' growth.

3. Which is *not* part of a portfolio?

    A. Samples of work selected by the student
    B. The student's self-assessment
    C. Cumulative folder information
    D. Progress notes from the teacher

4. Which is *not* a type of note in the portfolio?

    A. An evaluation for each piece of work
    B. Comments on use of some speech sounds
    C. Imitation of literature in this child's language
    D. How the child contributes in groups

5. Which does evaluation of writing *not* depend on?

    A. What the student wants to submit
    B. Particular genres or forms of writing emphasized
    C. Clearly stated criteria
    D. Comparisons to peers

6. Which is *not* an appropriate evaluation for third grade writing?

    A. Does the student use appropriate grammatical structures?
    B. Does the student use appropriate editing strategies?
    C. Are commas used properly?
    D. Does the student participate when writing is shared?

7. Which is *not* a valid reason for grouping?

    A. It provides more effective interactions.
    B. Students receive developmentally-appropriate instruction.
    C. It allows slower students to keep up.
    D. It improves the likelihood of appropriate instruction.

8. Which is *not* a reading performance level?

   A. Frustrational
   B. Correctional
   C. Instructional
   D. Independent

9. Which does the Informal Reading Inventory *not* assess?

   A. Comprehension levels
   B. Word analysis strategies
   C. Spelling
   D. Word analysis knowledge

10. Which does the Informal Reading Inventory *not* provide?

    A. Percentile information
    B. Word knowledge in context
    C. Comprehension in silent reading
    D. Comprehension in oral reading

11. During the Informal Reading Inventory the tester tunes into

    A. the taping process.
    B. expression during oral reading.
    C. growth from earlier readings.
    D. all of the above.

12. Which is *not* considered a miscue?

    A. Correction
    B. Insertion
    C. Substitution
    D. Stutter

13. A score of 88% on an informal spelling inventory indicates which instructional level?

    A. Frustrational
    B. Instructional
    C. Correctional
    D. Independent

14. Which type of standardized test score is *least* informative?

    A. Stanine
    B. Percentile
    C. Grade-equivalent
    D. Percentage

15. What type of information is obtained from an informal spelling inventory?

    A. A student's spelling instructional level
    B. Insights into a student's word knowledge
    C. A student's independent level in spelling
    D. All of the above

1. Which is *not* an informal assessment and evaluation purpose?

    A. Make comparisons of *large* groups.
    B. Determine student strengths.
    C. Help form groups.
    D. Determine how much children know.

2. Which is *not* an informal tool for assessment?

    A. Tape of oral reading
    B. Spelling inventory
    C. Unit test in the basal
    D. Cloze test on a history passage

3. Which is *not* part of a portfolio?

    A. Samples of works selected by the teacher
    B. Teacher observation notes
    C. Progress notes from the student
    D. Cumulative folder information

4. Which is *not* a type of note in the portfolio?

    A. How students express themselves through syntax and vocabulary
    B. How they rephrase when meaning is not clear
    C. A grade on each piece of writing
    D. How the student listens to others

5. Which is *not* an appropriate evaluation for third grade writing?

    A. Is the student serious while conferencing with peers?
    B. Can the student expand and combine sentences easily?
    C. Does the student use appropriate revision strategies?
    D. Are words used appropriately and effectively?

6. Which is *not* a part of informal reading assessment for grouping?

    A. Observe book choices during SSR.
    B. Observe willingness to predict in reading materials.
    C. Have the student read a passage orally.
    D. Administer a learning styles inventory.

7. Which is *not* a part of informal reading assessment for grouping?

    A. Administer the Durrell-Sullivan Phonic Test.
    B. Observe accuracy of predictions in DRTAs.
    C. Observe if the student can prove predictions from text.
    D. Observe reading rate.

8. Which is *not* true about an Informal Reading Inventory?

   A. It checks the strengths and weaknesses of all students.
   B. It is used with actual instructional materials.
   C. It compares a student to a normed population.
   D. It helps guide teachers in day-to-day instruction.

9. Which does the Informal Reading Inventory *not* provide?

   A. Word knowledge in isolation
   B. Grade placement information
   C. Comprehension in oral reading
   D. Oral reading fluency

10. During the Informal Reading Inventory, comprehension is checked by

    A. having the student retell the story.
    B. asking direct questions.
    C. probing student responses for expanding them.
    D. all of the above.

11. During the Informal Reading Inventory the tester tunes into

    A. word phrasing.
    B. the "naturalness" of the passage.
    C. the child's growth potential in reading.
    D. all of the above.

12. Which is *not* part of the reading portfolio?

    A. Attitudes about reading growth
    B. Responses to literature tasks
    C. Grades on specific tasks
    D. Progress in applying skills in meaningful reading

13. Which is *not* considered a miscue?

    A. Monotone
    B. Punctuation
    C. Repetition
    D. Omission

14. A score of 76% on an informal spelling inventory indicates which instructional level?

    A. Frustrational
    B. Instructional
    C. Correctional
    D. Independent

15. According to your text, which type of standardized test score is most misunderstood?

    A. Stanine
    B. Grade-equivalent
    C. Percentile
    D. Percentage

13

Diversity in the Language Arts Classroom

INSTRUCTIONAL OVERVIEW

CULTURALLY AND LINGUISTICALLY DIVERSE STUDENTS

Research on Success or Failure in School

Effects of Varied Literacy Experiences

Historical Perspectives on Second Language Education

    Challenges to Bilingual and ESL Programs

STUDENTS WITH SPECIAL EDUCATION NEEDS

Historical Perspectives on Special Education

Categories of Special Education in the Public Schools

STRATEGIES FOR INSTRUCTION

Classroom Organization and Overall Considerations

    Cooperative Groups
    Peer Tutoring
    Comprehensible Input

Reading

    Language Experience Approach
    Reading Aloud, "Narrow Reading," and Repeated Readings
    Critical Thinking and Problem Solving

Writing

    Dialogue Journals
    Computers

Thematic Units

Involving Parents

CHILDREN'S LITERATURE RELATED TO DIVERSITY

SUMMARY

All across the nation schools are faced with growing numbers of culturally and linguistically diverse students. Although California, Florida, New York, and Texas have larger populations of these students than other states, statistics indicate all teachers, at one time or another, will have culturally or linguistically different children in their classrooms. As a result, teachers must be prepared to teach these students. This involves not only knowing what teaching strategies to use, but also understanding and being sensitive to the changing "world" of these students. As stated by Basil Bernstein, "If the culture of the teacher is to become part of the consciousness of the child, then the culture of the child must first be in the consciousness of the teacher."

A great diversity exists among culturally and linguistically diverse students. Some are able to read and write in their first language and have considerable school experience. Usually they are able to transfer those skills quickly as they learn to read and write in English. Other students have had little or no experience with school and are not able to read or write in their native languages. Learning these skills in a second language is much more difficult for them.

Views about culturally and linguistically different people, the terminology used to describe them, and how they have been educated have undergone significant changes. Early in this century the concept of the "melting pot" prevailed. Students were expected to disregard and forget their native languages in order to achieve the goal of becoming an "American." Currently, cultural differences are recognized as being important and a strength for the individual; the concept of "American" has broadened to include the unique aspects of ethnic heritage. Terminology that was once considered appropriate is now considered offensive or unacceptable. Different explanations have been offered to account for the pessimistic statistics for the scholastic success of language minorities. Contextual interaction, which is currently widely accepted, suggests that there is no single answer to this phenomenon. One culture is not viewed as "superior" to another. Scholastic failure is attributed to a teaching and learning expectations mismatch between the teacher and the culturally and linguistically different child. Instruction for second language learners continues to be molded by political and philosophical beliefs. Controversy still exists about whether to meet instructional needs through bilingual programs or through English as a Second Language (ESL) programs.

Special education, like the education of minority language students, has undergone many changes. Until the 1960s little support existed for students with special needs. During that period, laws were passed that provided grants for teacher training, for education of children with special needs, and for resource centers to improve handicapped children's education. Additional laws expanded services to children deemed to be at risk from birth to age five. Mainstreaming was implemented and classification of exceptional students was revised. For the most part, teaching strategies for regular instruction are also appropriate for special needs students. Cooperative learning facilitates acceptance of diverse children and acquisition of concepts that are slightly beyond the student. Integrated, thematic units are particularly effective because children: 1) have many more opportunities to explore a concept; 2) more actively participate in their learning; and 3) are given the opportunity to explore a topic in depth. Peer tutoring and Krashen's concept of comprehensible input are also effective with diverse students. The LEA for reading instruction is appropriate for students of all ages. Narrow reading and repeated readings allow students to focus on specific aspects of reading and to use background knowledge more fully. Diverse students need good literature and to have their critical thinking and problem-solving skills developed. Writing is recommended for second language learners and special education students. Mastery of oral and written language is not required for beginning writing instruction. Self-selected topics, journal writing, dialogue writing, and computers encourage students to write. On a final note, it is very important that parents of special needs students be included in the educational process.

Books and stories that represent all cultures and deal with cultural, linguistic, academic, and physical differences are particularly important in classrooms with diverse students. Students need to realize that common themes and emotions are shared by all humans, regardless of their cultural backgrounds or physical or intellectual limitations. It is hoped, therefore, that children will focus on the similarities between people rather than on the differences.

SUPPLEMENTARY DISCUSSION TOPICS

1. In small groups let the students share and explain their cinquains. Then discuss the important points with the entire class.

2. First in small groups and then with the entire class, develop a semantic map of DIVERSE POPULATIONS. Discuss the terms and students' explanations of their groups of words.

3. Discuss Bernstein's quote, "If the culture of the teacher is to become part of the consciousness of the child, then the culture of the child must first be in the consciousness of the teacher." Brainstorm for ideas on how this can be accomplished.

4. Divide the class into two groups to debate the issue "ESL programs are more effective than bilingual ones." Have them research the topic and present their arguments.

5. Rather than study about culture (and serve tacos on Cinco de Mayo) an integrated language arts approach, as presented in this book, leads to an understanding of the children in the classroom and their culture. Discuss this difference with your students.

STUDENT ACTIVITIES

1. Have each student write a cinquain poem on this chapter. Follow the model for this poem as presented in earlier chapters or modify the lines to meet your needs.

2. Have your students observe in a classroom and look for student diversity. Have them describe the special needs children and explain why they consider them special. They can interview the teacher and have him/her identify those who have special needs. They should report the findings in a two-page paper.

3. Have your students observe some special needs children in a classroom and on the playground. Have them compare peer and adult interactions in both situations,

including their language, body language, demeanor, and so forth, and share findings in a two-page paper. The students are looking for differences between the classroom and playground behaviors.

4. Have your students interview a bilingual teacher, coordinator, or principal about how the needs are being met for second language learners. In a two-page paper, students can describe what they found out. Or, they can share the information with peers.

5. Have each student review the teachers' edition of a current reading/language arts text for suggestions offered for dealing with special needs children. Have them share and evaluate the ideas with peers; effective ideas may be added to students' teacher resource files.

6. Students can read at least three books listed in this chapter as suggestions for helping special needs children. They should take literary notes and add ideas for how this book might be used in the classroom. Students can share particularly effective ideas and add them to their teacher resource files.

1. Which is *not* appropriate for a second language learner?

    A. Read-alouds
    B. Sustained Silent Reading
    C. Strong skills component
    D. None of the above

2. Which probably transcends interests and styles of all learners?

    A. Intensive phonics instruction
    B. Good spelling skills
    C. Good literature
    D. All of the above

3. Which might reflect your future teaching situation?

    A. "If I stay out of California, I probably won't have to be concerned about variant populations in my classroom."
    B. "I will have some form of diversity in my classroom, no matter where I decide to teach."
    C. "Language problems of the new immigrants are very different from those of the last hundred years."
    D. "With all the special help for mainstreamed children, I don't have to be concerned with teaching special children."

4. An Individualized Educational Program

    A. does not have to specify how progress toward instructional objectives will be accomplished.
    B. is not required for students within certain special education categories.
    C. is becoming mandatory for all elementary students.
    D. must specify how instructional objectives must be met.

5. Students from which one of the following categories of special education are most likely to be represented in a regular education classroom?

    A. Low prevalence
    B. Hearing-impaired
    C. High prevalence
    D. None of the above

6. Which is *not* a valid conclusion based on the Heath and Wells studies of language learning for culturally different children?

    A. Success depends on matching the child's language with teacher expectation.
    B. Children with literacy skills in their own culture can have trouble in school.
    C. The literacy developed at home is inappropriate for instruction at school.
    D. Teachers must be conscious of the child's culture.

7. Which is *not* a part of ESL classes?

   A. Brief instruction in a few English phrases
   B. Strong support for culture background
   C. Classroom instruction in the English language
   D. Special support only briefly each day

8. Which is *not* a problem for second language learners?

   A. They have difficulty thinking abstractly in the English language.
   B. They may never catch up in content.
   C. They become fluent in two languages.
   D. All of the above.

9. LEA is so powerful for special needs populations because

   A. it helps the learner deal with emotional problems.
   B. it allows the older learners to read appropriate content.
   C. it uses the language of the child.
   D. all of the above.

10. Which is *not* an appropriate activity for special needs learners?

    A. Word etymology
    B. Narrow reading
    C. Read-alouds
    D. Repeated reading

11. Which accounts for special needs students performing beyond their individual competence?

    A. Zone of proximal development
    B. Repeated reading
    C. Narrow reading
    D. Zone of cognitive awareness

12. Which is *not* a way of developing critical thinking in special needs learners?

    A. Ask mostly higher-level comprehension questions.
    B. Give a concrete example for an abstract concept.
    C. Provide concrete manipulation for abstract concepts.
    D. Predict before they read.

13. Which is *not* true for why dialogue journals are powerful for special needs learners?

    A. They reduce distance between teacher and student.
    B. They are easy to grade.
    C. The learner is the initiator.
    D. The writing is communicative.

14. Which is *not* a feature of thematic units for special needs learners?

    A. Central topic deeply explored
    B. Differentiated roles for slower learners
    C. Binary-opposite concepts
    D. Narrow reading

15. Which is *not* an especially effective use of computers for special needs learners?

    A. Interactive stories requiring problem-solving skills
    B. Group revision and editing of a class newsletter
    C. Pairing students for story writing
    D. Workbook-type skill activities for reading development

1. Which is *not* appropriate for a learning-handicapped child?

    A. Language experiences
    B. Journal writing
    C. Intensive skills work
    D. None of the above

2. Which is probably appropriate with any special needs learner?

    A. Report writing
    B. Good literature
    C. Spelling instruction at grade level
    D. All of the above

3. Which might reflect your future teaching situation?

    A. "If I get immigrant children in my classroom, they may or may not be literate in their native language."
    B. "No matter where they come from, my students must fit the mainstream ideal of a good American citizen."
    C. "Immigrants have to learn to speak our language quickly, so they fit in with the rest of the students."
    D. None of the above.

4. Which is currently *not* an acceptable label?

    A. First language student
    B. Culturally disadvantaged
    C. Second language student
    D. All of the above

5. Non-English-speaking parents who are nonliterate in their native language may best help their children acquire concepts about literacy through

    A. sharing wordless books with the children.
    B. taking dictation from their children.
    C. reassuring their children that the teacher will teach them everything they need to know.
    D. encouraging their children to watch educational television programs.

6. Students who exaggerate the facts when they retell an event are probably

    A. trying to direct attention away from themselves.
    B. unfamiliar with stories.
    C. experiencing difficulties with reading comprehension.
    D. following a pattern that is common in their own cultural group.

7. The text suggests that, in order for culturally and/or linguistically diverse students to learn about the mainstream culture,

   A. they should be totally immersed in it as soon as possible.
   B. the culture of the students must be in the consciousness of the teacher.
   C. the teacher should try to have available as much material as possible that represents aspects of the mainstream culture.
   D. the culture of the teacher must somehow be in the consciousness of the student.

8. Which is *not* a part of bilingual classes?

   A. They are taught by a bilingual teacher.
   B. Students are taught a few key phrases.
   C. They are taught in the primary language and concurrently with English.
   D. The students are isolated from their age-mates for a long time.

9. LEA is so powerful for special needs populations because

   A. it provides a bridge from oral language to the other language arts.
   B. the learner shares personal experiences.
   C. sharing is generally done individually or in small groups.
   D. all of the above.

10. Which is *not* an appropriate activity for special needs learners?

    A. Read-alouds
    B. Repeated readings
    C. Copying the text from a newspaper comic strip
    D. Picture books

11. Cooperative learning in small groups promotes speech development in second language learners because

    A. the sheltered atmosphere is conducive to speech.
    B. each member must contribute ideas.
    C. group members can clarify meaning through drawing.
    D. all of the above.

12. For zone of proximal development to work, a special needs learner's knowledge must be

    A. considerably below the group's level of discussion.
    B. slightly below the group's level of discussion.
    C. considerably above the group's level of discussion.
    D. slightly above the group's level of discussion.

13. Which activity does *not* help special needs learners write?

    A. Delay writing until oral and reading skills are developed.
    B. Ignore spelling and grammar errors.
    C. Don't point out mixed language encoding.
    D. Encourage them to write what they know and feel.

14. Which is *not* an especially effective use of computers for special needs learners?

   A. Keyboarding
   B. Paired-group story writing
   C. Interactive stories
   D. Modem communication

15. When working with diverse learners, the development of critical thinking skills

   A. should be delayed until the students have mastered oral English.
   B. is only appropriate with students literate in their first language.
   C. aids the development of reading and writing skills.
   D. is only appropriate for students in the fourth through sixth grades.

ANSWERS TO TEST ITEMS

Answer Sheet for Exam 1-A

Test Question	Correct Answer
1	D
2	D
3	C
4	C
5	C
6	D
7	C
8	A
9	A
10	C
11	C
12	A
13	B
14	A
15	B

Answer Sheet for Exam 2-A

Test Question	Correct Answer
1	A
2	A
3	C
4	B
5	D
6	B
7	A
8	A
9	B
10	B
11	D
12	B
13	C
14	D
15	C

Answer Sheet for Exam 1-B

Test Question	Correct Answer
1	C
2	D
3	C
4	B
5	A
6	C
7	D
8	A
9	B
10	D
11	C
12	A
13	C
14	B
15	B

Answer Sheet for Exam 2-B

Test Question	Correct Answer
1	B
2	B
3	D
4	B
5	A
6	A
7	D
8	A
9	C
10	B
11	B
12	C
13	D
14	A
15	D

Answer Sheet for Exam 3-A

Test Question	Correct Answer
1	D
2	B
3	C
4	A
5	B
6	C
7	A
8	B
9	D
10	B
11	B
12	C
13	A
14	D
15	D

Answer Sheet for Exam 4-A

Test Question	Correct Answer
1	D
2	A
3	B
4	C
5	C
6	A
7	D
8	B
9	D
10	A
11	C
12	C
13	A
14	B
15	D

Answer Sheet for Exam 3-B

Test Question	Correct Answer
1	D
2	A
3	C
4	D
5	B
6	D
7	D
8	B
9	C
10	A
11	C
12	B
13	A
14	C
15	A

Answer Sheet for Exam 4-B

Test Question	Correct Answer
1	A
2	D
3	C
4	D
5	A
6	B
7	C
8	B
9	C
10	D
11	B
12	B
13	D
14	C
15	C

Answer Sheet for Exam 5-A

Test Question	Correct Answer
1	B
2	D
3	D
4	A
5	B
6	D
7	C
8	D
9	A
10	B
11	B
12	D
13	D
14	A
15	C

Answer Sheet for Exam 6-A

Test Question	Correct Answer
1	C
2	A
3	B
4	C
5	B
6	D
7	A
8	A
9	D
10	D
11	A
12	B
13	B
14	C
15	B

Answer Sheet for Exam 5-B

Test Question	Correct Answer
1	D
2	A
3	A
4	D
5	C
6	D
7	C
8	D
9	D
10	C
11	B
12	A
13	A
14	D
15	B

Answer Sheet for Exam 6-B

Test Question	Correct Answer
1	A
2	B
3	D
4	C
5	B
6	B
7	A
8	C
9	A
10	D
11	B
12	C
13	D
14	C
15	D

Answer Sheet for Exam 7-A

Test Question	Correct Answer
1	A
2	D
3	B
4	A
5	B
6	A
7	C
8	D
9	D
10	C
11	B
12	C
13	C
14	A
15	D

Answer Sheet for Exam 8-A

Test Question	Correct Answer
1	C
2	D
3	B
4	D
5	B
6	D
7	A
8	C
9	D
10	C
11	A
12	A
13	B
14	B
15	B

Answer Sheet for Exam 7-B

Test Question	Correct Answer
1	A
2	D
3	A
4	B
5	B
6	C
7	D
8	A
9	C
10	C
11	C
12	D
13	D
14	B
15	A

Answer Sheet for Exam 8-B

Test Question	Correct Answer
1	A
2	D
3	D
4	D
5	B
6	D
7	C
8	A
9	C
10	B
11	D
12	D
13	B
14	D
15	A

Answer Sheet for Exam 9-A

Test Question	Correct Answer
1	B
2	B
3	D
4	C
5	D
6	A
7	B
8	C
9	A
10	B
11	C
12	D
13	C
14	A
15	C

Answer Sheet for Exam 10-A

Test Question	Correct Answer
1	D
2	A
3	A
4	A
5	D
6	C
7	B
8	B
9	A
10	B
11	D
12	C
13	C
14	B
15	D

Answer Sheet for Exam 9-B

Test Question	Correct Answer
1	B
2	D
3	B
4	D
5	C
6	B
7	A
8	A
9	A
10	D
11	C
12	C
13	C
14	B
15	A

Answer Sheet for Exam 10-B

Test Question	Correct Answer
1	D
2	B
3	D
4	D
5	A
6	C
7	B
8	C
9	A
10	C
11	B
12	A
13	B
14	A
15	C

Answer Sheet for Exam 11-A

Test Question	Correct Answer
1	A
2	B
3	D
4	C
5	D
6	B
7	A
8	C
9	C
10	B
11	D
12	A
13	D
14	A
15	C

Answer Sheet for Exam 12-A

Test Question	Correct Answer
1	D
2	B
3	C
4	A
5	D
6	A
7	C
8	B
9	C
10	A
11	B
12	D
13	B
14	C
15	D

Answer Sheet for Exam 11-B

Test Question	Correct Answer
1	C
2	A
3	B
4	D
5	A
6	B
7	D
8	C
9	B
10	A
11	D
12	C
13	B
14	B
15	D

Answer Sheet for Exam 12-B

Test Question	Correct Answer
1	A
2	C
3	D
4	C
5	B
6	D
7	A
8	C
9	B
10	D
11	A
12	C
13	A
14	B
15	B

Answer Sheet for Exam 13-A

Test Question	Correct Answer
1	D
2	C
3	B
4	D
5	C
6	C
7	B
8	C
9	D
10	A
11	A
12	A
13	B
14	B
15	D

Answer Sheet for Exam 13-B

Test Question	Correct Answer
1	D
2	B
3	A
4	B
5	A
6	D
7	B
8	B
9	D
10	C
11	A
12	B
13	A
14	A
15	C

PART TWO

INSTRUCTIONAL MASTERS

INSTRUCTIONAL MASTERS

These instructional masters may be used to make overhead transparencies for lectures and/or handouts to accompany your class presentation. Following is a list of masters with suggestions for use:

Master #1 ("Before Reading This Text"): This master is based on the "No-Book DRTA" developed by J. Thomas Gill and Donald Bear.* You may use it to tap into your students' background knowledge during the very first class meeting. They will immediately become more involved in the subject matter. You may have the students work through this individually, in groups, or combine both individual and group work (for example, #1 would be done individually, and students would work in small groups beginning with item #2).

Master #2 ("The History of English: Overview"): Showing the approximate dates for the Old, Middle, and Modern English periods, this transparency is meant to be used as part of the introduction to your lecture or discussion about the history of the English language.

Masters #3a and 3b ("The History of English"): Providing important benchmark dates, these two masters may be used to "anchor" your discussion of English.

Master #4 ("Functions of Language"): This master may be used in lectures and discussion for both Chapters 2 and 5. You may fill in examples for each function and/or elicit these from the students. For example, after reading and discussing about the functions of language in the preschool years, students could suggest examples illustrating each function for the elementary school years.

Master #5 ("Discussion Group Basics"): Taken from the guidelines in Chapter 5, this master may be used at any point in the course, particularly whenever you break the class into small discussion groups.

Master #6 ("Cinquain Format"): As mentioned in the first part of this manual, you may have the students construct cinquains as a means of organizing their knowledge about a topic. This transparency will allow you to teach this format, constructing on the overhead projector a sample cinquain.

Master #7 ("Genre Schemes"): There is a considerable, though necessary, number of terms introduced beginning in Chapter 6 that describe writing and reading. This transparency should come in handy not only for introducing these major concepts but for maintaining a clear focus on the most significant terms and concepts.

Master #8 ("The Writing Process"): This should be a handy reference throughout your discussions regarding the teaching of writing.

Master #9 ("Amelia Earhart"): This short passage provides the "text" for modeling Question-Answer Relationships in Chapter 8. You may also wish to use this during Chapter 6 to help students realize the distinctions among literal, inferential, and critical comprehension.

Masters #10a and 10b ("Question-Answer Relationships"): There is one example from each of the "QAR" categories: "Right There" and "Put it Together" are "In the Book"-type questions, and "Author and You" and "On My Own" are "In My Head"-type questions.

Master #11 ("Semantic Feature Analysis"): This master will provide a handy introduction or review for types and formats of writing (Chapters 6 and 7) as well as an example of this type of vocabulary instructional technique as presented in Chapter 10.

Masters #12a and 12b ("Word Sorts: Diphthong /oy/"): Providing a "pre" and "post" example of a word sort presented in the text, these overheads should help your students get a feel for the kinds of understandings and awarenesses about words that can develop as a consequence of doing word sorts. Show them the first transparency, and ask them to sort the words into two columns: one in which the /oy/ sound is spelled *oi* and one in which the sound is spelled *oy*. This sort should result in an arrangement similar to the one shown on transparency #12b. Then ask them to examine the two columns in order to determine the conditions under which /oy/ is spelled *oi* or *oy*.

Master #13 ("The Spelling/Meaning Connection"): This transparency should help you illustrate one type of spelling/meaning relationship. The word pairs each provide an example of how a stressed vowel in one word can be a clue to the spelling of the schwa in the related word. These examples help your students grasp this concept, which the text describes as follows: "Words that are related in meaning are often related in spelling as well, despite changes in sound."

Masters #14a, 14b, 14c, and 14d ("Developmental Stages"): Each of these four transparencies provides a brief summary of the significant characteristics of literacy behaviors at different developmental levels. 14a presents characteristics of children who are developing a concept of word in print; 14b is "Letter Name," representing those behaviors that characterize children who are ready to begin *conventional* literacy instruction; 14c is "Within Word Pattern," where children are moving towards fluency in reading and in writing; and 14d combines the stages characterized by "syllable juncture" and "derivational relationships" word knowledge, where reading and writing are fluent. You will find these transparencies helpful when discussing the development of reading and writing in Chapter 6 as well as in Chapter 7 (writing) and Chapter 8 (reading).

---

*Gill, J.T. & Bear, D. (1988). No-book, whole-book and chapter DRTAs. *Journal of Reading, 31,* 444–449.

Before Reading This Text . . .

1. LIST EVERYTHING YOU CAN THINK OF THAT MIGHT BE IN A BOOK ON THE SUBJECT "TEACHING THE INTEGRATED LANGUAGE ARTS"

2. PUT ITEMS LISTED ABOVE INTO GROUPS.

3. GIVE EACH GROUP A NAME, AND ARRANGE A TABLE OF CONTENTS.

4. NOW CHECK THE TABLE OF CONTENTS, AND NOTICE HOW MUCH YOUR LIST CORRESPONDS TO THE BOOK!

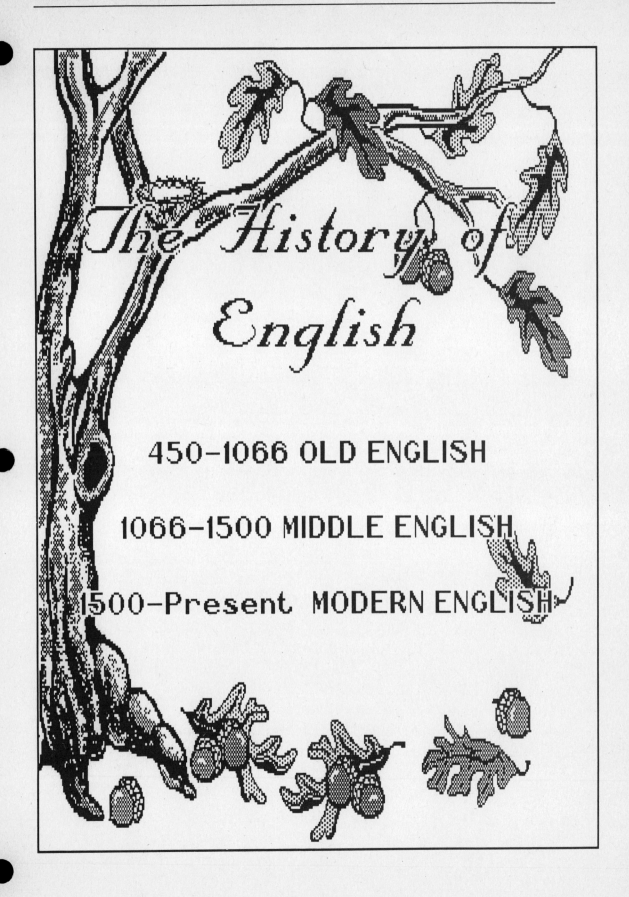

The History of English

450–1066 OLD ENGLISH

1066–1500 MIDDLE ENGLISH

1500–Present MODERN ENGLISH

The History of English

450 A.D. ROMANS LEAVE;
                ANGLES/JUTES/
                SAXONS SOON INVADE

750   DANISH INVASION

1000   ENGLISH "LANGUAGE
                OF INTELLECTUALS"
                THROUGHOUT EUROPE

1066   NORMAN INVASION

C. 1400   CHAUCER'S
            "CANTERBURY TALES"

1476   RENAISSANCE;
        PRINTING PRESS

1500's "VOYAGES OF
            DISCOVERY"

1564– WILLIAM SHAKESPEARE
1616

1755   SAMUEL JOHNSON'S
          DICTIONARY

1828   NOAH WEBSTER'S
          DICTIONARY

Functions of Language

INSTRUMENTAL:

REGULATORY:

INTERACTIONAL:

PERSONAL:

IMAGINATIVE:

HEURISTIC:

INFORMATIVE:

DISCUSSION GROUP BASICS

1. DECIDE WHAT THE QUESTION TO BE DISCUSSED MEANS; DISCUSS MEANING WITH GROUP.
2. MAKE SURE GROUP DECIDES ON ONE MEANING.
3. SAY YOUR OWN IDEAS.
4. LISTEN TO OTHERS; GIVE EVERYONE A CHANCE TO TALK.
5. ASK OTHERS FOR THEIR IDEAS.
6. GIVE REASONS FOR YOUR IDEAS AND DISCUSS MANY DIFFERENT IDEAS.

Cinquain Format

NOUN:

TWO
ADJECTIVES:

THREE WORDS
EXPRESSING
ACTION:

FOUR WORDS
EXPRESSING
FEELING:

NOUN:

GENRE SCHEMES:

NARRATIVE

NARRATION   POETRY

EXPOSITORY

EXPRESSION
DESCRIPTION
EXPOSITION
PERSUASION

THE WRITING PROCESS

PREWRITING

DRAFTING

REVISING

EDITING

SHARING AND PUBLISHING

IN 1937, AMELIA EARHART SET
OUT WITH HER NAVIGATOR, PETER
NOONAN, TO FLY AROUND THE
WORLD. HER TWIN-ENGINE PLANE
WAS LOST SOMEWHERE BETWEEN
NEW GUINEA AND HOWLAND ISLE.
WE MAY NEVER KNOW WHAT BECAME
OF AMELIA EARHART--WHETHER
SHE PERISHED IN THE PACIFIC
OCEAN OR, AS SOME SUGGEST,
MET HER FATE ON LAND.
REGARDLESS, SHE WILL ALWAYS
REMAIN AN INSPIRATION TO THOSE
WHO BELIEVE IN TRULY STRIVING
TO REACH THEIR DREAMS.

Question-Answer Relationships

1. WHEN DID AMELIA EARHART SET
   OUT TO FLY AROUND
     THE WORLD?
       (ANSWER IS "RIGHT THERE.")

2. WAS AMELIA EARHART ALONE
   ON HER FLIGHT?
   (YOU HAVE TO "PUT IT
   TOGETHER" TO ANSWER THIS.)

Question-Answer Relationships

3. DID AMELIA EARHART DISAPPEAR BEFORE OR AFTER THE SECOND WORLD WAR?
   ("AUTHOR AND YOU": IF YOU KNOW WHEN THE SECOND WORLD WAR OCCURRED, THEN YOU HAVE ENOUGH INFORMATION TO ANSWER THE QUESTION.)
4. DID CONGRESS WANT TO LAUNCH AN INVESTIGATION INTO THE DISAPPEARANCE?
   (ANSWER IS AN "ON MY OWN" TYPE BECAUSE THERE ISN'T ENOUGH TEXT INFORMATION.)

SEMANTIC FEATURE ANALYSIS

	STAND ON ITS OWN	GET THINGS DONE	EGO-CENTRIC
STORY			
ESSAY			
SONNET			
BALLAD			
EDITORIAL			
NOVEL			

SOIL	HOIST
TOY	ANNOY
REJOICE	DECOY
BOYCOTT	EXPLOIT
POISON	VOYAGE
SPOIL	EMBROIDER
EMPLOY	LOYAL

SOIL	TOY
HOIST	ANNOY
REJOICE	DECOY
EXPLOIT	BOYCOTT
EMBROIDER	VOYAGE
POISON	EMPLOY
SPOIL	LOYAL

COMPETE
COMPETITION

PRESIDE
PRESIDENT

LEGAL
LEGALITY

NORMAL
NORMALITY

Reading

CONCEPT OF WORD IN PRINT
(VOICE/PRINT MATCH)

Writing

SLOW; ABLE TO PRODUCE
"DECODABLE" STRINGS OF
CONSONANTS

Word Knowledge

SEMIPHONEMIC:
PNK (PINK); BD (BED); DF (DRIVE)

Voice

EXPRESSIVE (EGOCENTRIC)

Reading

WORD-BY-WORD ORAL READING

Writing

WORD-BY-WORD, INVENT
SPELLINGS LETTER BY LETTER

Word Knowledge

LETTER NAME (PHONEMIC):
FES (FISH); CHRAN (TRAIN)

Voice

EXPRESSIVE

Reading

TOWARD FLUENCY AND EXPRESSION

Writing

TOWARD FLUENCY; WORDS ENCODED IN GROUPS OF LETTERS

Word Knowledge

WITHIN-WORD PATTERN: TRANE (TRAIN); DRIEV (DRIVE)

Voice

TRANSACTIONAL AND POETIC

Reading

FLUENCY AND EXPRESSION;
ADJUST TO FIT PURPOSES

Writing

FLUENT; "IN CONTROL"

Word Knowledge

SYLLABLE JUNCTURE:
SUDEN (SUDDEN); DISSAPEAR
DERIVATIONAL CONSTANCY:
BENIFIT; ATRACT

Voice

TRANSACTIONAL AND POETIC

Instructor Evaluation of TEACHING THE INTEGRATED LANGUAGE ARTS

Please complete the questionnaire and mail it to: Marketing Services, College Division, Houghton Mifflin Company, One Beacon Street, Boston, MA 02108.

1. We would like to know how you rate our textbook in each of the following areas:

		Excellent	Good	Adequate	Poor
a.	Selection of topics	___	___	___	___
b.	Detail of coverage	___	___	___	___
c.	Order of topics	___	___	___	___
d.	Writing style/reading ability	___	___	___	___
e.	Accuracy of information	___	___	___	___
f.	Study aids and Resource lists	___	___	___	___
g.	Usefulness of activities and Classroom Examples	___	___	___	___
h.	Value of *At the Teacher's Desk* feature	___	___	___	___
i.	Student reactions to book	___	___	___	___
j.	Value of figures and photographs	___	___	___	___
k.	Explanation of concepts	___	___	___	___

2. We invite you to cite specific examples that illustrate any of the above ratings.

_____

_____

_____

3. Describe the strongest feature(s) of the book.

_____

_____

_____

4. Describe the weakest feature(s) of the book.

_____

_____

_____

5. What other topics, if any, should be included in this text?

_____

_____

_____

6. Do you use the book as part of an undergraduate course? _____ graduate course? _____ workshop? _____ both undergraduate and graduate courses? _____

7a. What is the title of the course in which the book is used? _____
_____

7b. Is it a course in Language Arts Education or a combined course in Reading and Language Arts? _____

8. How does our book compare with others that are available for the course?

           <u>Book Title</u>   <u>Comparison</u>

a. _____   _____
                                             _____

b. _____   _____
                                             _____

c. _____   _____
                                             _____

9. In terms of the following features of the instructor's manual:

a. Did you in any way use the Discussion Outline included in the manual?
Yes _____ No _____

b. Did you in any way use the Summaries included in the manual?
Yes _____ No _____

c. Did you in any way use the Test Items given in the manual?
Yes _____ No _____

d. Did you in any way use the activity suggestions included in the manual?
Yes _____ No _____

e. Did you in any way use the Masters given in the manual?
Yes _____ No _____

f. We invite explanations of the answers you have given about the instructor's manual and an overall evaluation of its usefulness.

10. Do you intend to use the text again? _____